SPELLING RULES!

Makes spelling stick!

Helen Pearson and Janelle Ho

BOOK

D

Name: _____

Class: _____

Gill & Macmillan

CONTENTS

Gill & Macmillan

Hume Avenue

Park West

Dublin 12

with associated companies throughout the world

www.gillmacmillan.ie

© Helen Pearson, Janelle Ho, 2009

978 07171 4586 7

Advisor: Alison MacMahon

Design by Trish Hayes and Stephen Michael King

Illustrations by Stephen Michael King

SCOPE AND SEQUENCE

Unit	Page	Skill focus					
		Vowels	Consonants	Letter patterns	Morphology and etymology	Homophones/ Confusing words	Topic words
1	6	a-e, i-e					
2	8	o-e, u-e					shapes
3	10	oo, ee, ea, ai, oa					
4	12			ow, ou, oy, ey, ay			
5	14				words beginning with a-, al-, un-, dis-		
6	16	REVISION					
7	18				adding -s, -ed, -ing, -ly		
8	20				proper nouns, apostrophes of possession		
9	22				-er, -est		
10	24	ie				peace/piece, cheap/cheep	
11	26				un-, mis-, dis-		
12	28	REVISION					
13	30						Christmas
14	32				-ful: changing y to i		
15	34		words ending in ss		-less: changing y to i		
16	36		medial double consonants				
17	38		silent letters: kn, wr	le			
18	40				capital letters for proper nouns		months of the year
19	42	REVISION					
20	44			igh, eigh			
21	46			ough, augh			antonyms
22	48				-ness, -ion, -ship, -dom, -hood, -ward		
23	50	words ending in o, oe			irregular plurals	there/their/they're	
24	52		words ending in f, ff, fe, ffe		-s: changing f to v		collective nouns
25	54	REVISION					
26	56		silent letters		non-English words		
27	58		soft and hard c: soft c before e, i, y				
28	60		soft and hard g: soft g before e, i, y				
29	62			qu		quit/quiet/quite	
30	64				uni-, bi-, tri-, kilo-, dec-, centi-, milli-		measurement
31	66	REVISION					
32	68			ble, gle, tle, cle, kle, dle			
33	70			ion			
34	72				non-English words	desert/dessert, course/coarse	
35	74	REVISION OF UNITS 1-34					

NOTE TO TEACHERS AND PARENTS

Spelling Rules!
A whole-school spelling programme that makes spelling stick!

Some students are natural spellers. They seem to become proficient spellers without any explicit instruction. But the vast majority of students need formal, systematic and sequential instruction about the way spelling works and the strategies they can use to become independent, confident spellers and spelling risk-takers.

The *Spelling Rules!* programme is based on sound linguistic and pedagogical theory. It is informed by recent research into how students of different ages acquire and apply spelling skills, and how those skills move from the working to the long-term memory. The programme consists of five books.

Spelling knowledge

Learning to spell involves developing different kinds of spelling knowledge:

☆ **Kinaesthetic knowledge**—the physical feeling when saying different sounds and words, and when writing the shapes of letters and words.

☆ **Phonological knowledge**—how a word sounds and the patterns of sounds in words.

☆ **Visual knowledge**—how letters and words look and the visual patterns in words.

☆ **Morphemic knowledge**—the meaning or function of words or parts of words.

☆ **Etymological knowledge**—the origins and history of words and the effect this has on spelling patterns.

Icons used in Book D

The following icons identify the main spelling strategy that students will use to complete an activity.

Say the word. (Kinaesthetic knowledge) These activities ask students to experience how sounds feel in the mouth and jaw. Changing the positions of the jaw, lips, and tongue changes the sounds we make. Encourage students to pronounce the sounds and words accurately. If they mispronounce a sound or word, they may misrepresent it in writing.

Listen to the word. (Phonological knowledge) These activities focus on discriminating between different sounds and breaking up words into syllables or individual sound segments (phonemes).

Look at the word. (Visual knowledge) These activities help students to see how the sound is represented using combinations of letters, and to associate this visual pattern with what they are hearing. Students will develop the ability to know when a word does or does not 'look right'.

Understand the word. (Morphemic and etymological knowledge) These activities focus on word meanings, word families, prefixes and suffixes, spelling rules, word origins and so on—all of which help embed spelling in the long-term memory.

Practise writing the word. (Kinaesthetic knowledge) These activities develop students' awareness of the physical movement involved in writing the word. By practising writing the word a number of times and in different contexts, the spelling becomes embedded in the long-term memory.

Rule! This icon highlights useful spelling rules. The rule is always introduced the first time students will need it to complete an activity. There is also a handy summary of important rules on page 80.

Tip! This icon tells students that a special clue or hint is provided for an activity. It may be a spelling, grammar or punctuation convention, or a definition of a useful term.

Book D

UNITS OF WORK

Book D contains 35 weekly units of work. See the **Scope and Sequence chart** on page 3 for more information.

WORD LISTS

Spelling lists enable a spelling element to be focused on. And they provide sufficient examples to consolidate the teaching point. In *Book D*, each unit (except Revision) has a list of twelve spelling words. The core words in the lists have been chosen to support the learning focus and strategies being taught in the unit. In addition, some words that can be confusing and topic words are introduced. The words are listed in order from simplest to more challenging.

SLLURP

Each word list begins with a reminder for students to SLLURP. SLLURP summarises the strategies that will help spelling move from students' working memory to their long-term memory.

Say the word carefully and slowly to yourself.
Listen to how each part of the word sounds in sequence.
Look at the patterns of letters in the word and the shape of the word.
Understand rules, word meanings and word origins.
Remember all the similar words you can already spell and relate this knowledge to any new word.
Practise writing the word until it is firmly fixed in your long-term memory.

List words support the learning of the spelling focus for the unit

SLLURP reminds students about strategies they can use to learn the words

Unit banner features the spelling focus in the context of an amazing fact

Sequenced activities— each activity focuses on a specific spelling strategy

Space to practise list words; to write theme words, personal words or extension words; or to practise other words with the same spelling focus. Adapt this section to suit the needs of your class

Icons identify the main spelling strategy students will use in an activity

Spelling tips and rules introduced when students need them to complete an activity

Spelling focus highlighted in colour

Footer shows the spelling focus for the unit

Tapeworms can live inside people. They can be up to 25 metres long — that's the length of two buses!

Say Listen Look Understand Remember Practise
care _____
made _____
table _____
place _____
shade _____
awake _____
time _____
slice _____
stripe _____
while _____
white _____
alive _____

1 Find a list word that rhymes. Write another word that follows the pattern.

space _____ _____

price _____ _____

fade _____ _____

snake _____ _____

cable _____ _____

smile _____ _____

drive _____ _____

quite _____ _____

share _____ _____

2 Write an **a-e** word to match each meaning.

f _ _ _   the front of your head

sh _ _ _   you don't do this if you have a beard

sn _ _ _   a reptile with no legs

br _ _ _   willing to face danger

3 Write an **i-e** word to match each meaning.

sl _ _ _   slip downwards

pr _ _ _   what something costs

m _ _ _   more than one mouse

in _ _ _ _   not outside

Rule! For most verbs ending in **e**, you drop the **e** before adding **ed** to make the past tense.   *live → lived*

But be careful – some verbs do not follow this rule!

make → made   *drive → drove*

4 Complete each sentence by writing the verb in the past tense.

Everyone _____ the concert yesterday.
       like

I once had a dog _____ Buddy.
                  name

Simon _____ on the wet leaves and hurt his foot.
       slide

Eddie _____ goodbye as his mum drove off.
       wave

Dad _____ me ten euro on my last birthday.
      give

Rule! Most nouns ending in **e** make the plural by adding **s**.

5 Write the plural for each noun.

cave _____   gate _____   race _____

fire _____   line _____   side _____

6 Say each word out loud. Change the short vowel to a long vowel by adding **e**.

din _____   rat _____   pin _____

fat _____   strip _____   tap _____

7 Colour the correct word.

Boil the eggs in a | pan | pane | of water.

Our | car | care | was parked for too long and we got a | fin | fine |.

Tomatoes turn red when they are | rip | ripe |.

May I | rid | ride | my bike to the park?

Unit 2

The funny bone is not actually a bone. It is a nerve behind your elbow.

home _____
stone _____
close _____
whole _____
alone _____
gone _____
love _____
done _____
use _____
pure _____
huge _____
cube _____

1 Words can rhyme but be spelt differently. Find a list word that rhymes.

knows	toes	_____
won	sun	_____
choose	news	_____
bone	moan	_____
foal	bowl	_____
dove	shove	_____
shone	upon	_____
foam	dome	_____

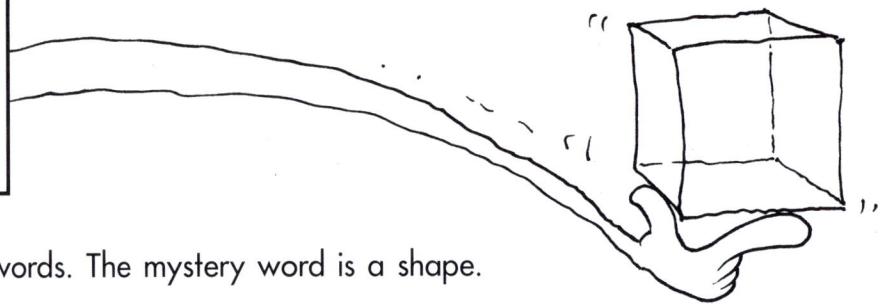

2 Use the clues to find list words. The mystery word is a shape.

1. not spoilt or dirty
2. I _ _ _ _ you!
3. Please _ _ _ _ _ the door.
4. a piece of rock
5. all by yourself
6. Have you _ _ _ _ your work?
7. past tense of 'go'
8. complete
9. an object with six square sides

Mystery word: _____

3 👁 There are many ways to say *big*. Arrange these words in alphabetical order.

huge   large   giant   big   enormous   great

_____

4 🦻 Syllables are the beats in a word. Write how many syllables you hear in each shape word.

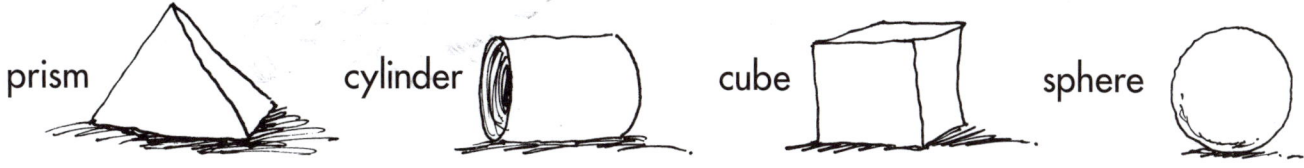

prism   cylinder   cube   sphere

5 😁 Say each word out loud. Change the short vowel to a long vowel by adding **e**.

tub _____   rod _____   hop _____

cub _____   hug _____   us _____

⭐ **Tip!**   **Homophones** are words that sound the same but are spelt differently.

---

6 👁 Colour the correct homophone.

This field is full of lambs and | ewes | use |.

The | whole | hole | we dug is now full of muddy water.

Are you | shore | sure | this is the right way home?

7 ✏️ Each set of words has the same spelling pattern, but one word sounds different.
Circle the one with a different sound and then use it in your own sentence.

sure	_____
pure	_____
cure	_____

dove	_____
love	_____
move	_____

Unit 3

It is easier to fl**oa**t in sea water than in fresh water.

Say Listen Look Understand Remember Practise

t**oo**l	_____
sh**oo**k	_____
bl**oo**d	_____
str**ee**t	_____
sw**ee**p	_____
dr**ea**m	_____
h**ea**d	_____
b**ea**ch	_____
gr**ea**t	_____
p**ai**nt	_____
r**oa**d	_____
fl**oa**t	_____

1 Find a list word that rhymes.

school	flood	crook
_____	_____	_____
scream	dead	wait
_____	_____	_____
faint	vote	showed
_____	_____	_____

2 Add another word to make a compound word.

door _____   tooth _____

moon _____   _____ spoon

broom _____   _____ room

3 Write the word in the plural.

beach _____   street _____   tooth _____

year _____   goose _____   groan _____

4 Add the correct suffix to these words. Choose from **s**, **ed**, or **ing**.

Dad is sweep_____ the leaves from the driveway.

The wind blew my hat into the water. Luckily it float_____ .

I hope we see a rainbow when the sun break _____ through the clouds.

After our homework we feast _____ on hot toast with butter.

10   Vowel digraphs oo, ee, ea, ai, oa

A **noun** names something. *roof, wood, fear, soap*

A **verb** is an action word. *cook, float, leave, sleep*

Some words can be nouns and verbs. *I have a **fear** of spiders.* (noun)

*I **fear** the worst.* (verb)

5 Is the underlined word used as a noun or a verb?

_____ Amy had a bad <u>dream</u> and woke up crying.

_____ Mix red and white <u>paint</u> to make pink.

_____ The striker tried to <u>boot</u> the soccer ball into the net.

_____ I gave a loud <u>scream</u> when the door slammed.

_____ We heard our puppy <u>moan</u> in his sleep.

6 Colour the correct homophone.

I need | to | too | two | eggs to make a cake.

Samantha is | to | too | two | sick to come | to | too | two | the party.

May I watch television | to | too | two | ?

Our car needs new | breaks | brakes |.

Fiona | rowed | road | two kilometres down the river.

7 Add a letter to make a new word. Use the clue!

heat → _____ (grain used to make flour)

beat → _____ (wild animal)

read → _____ (...! Steady! Go!)

Unit 4

Bamboo can grow up to 91 cm in one day.

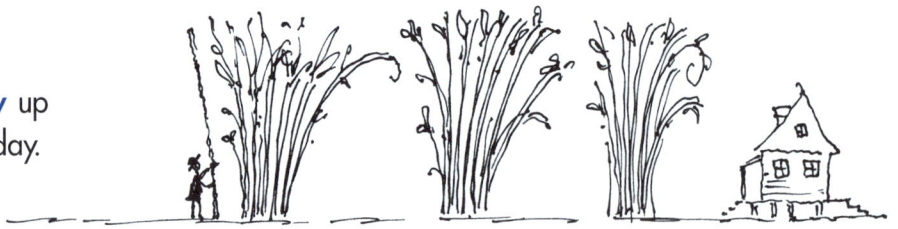

grow	_____
throw	_____
below	_____
ground	_____
found	_____
proud	_____
mountain	_____
enjoy	_____
money	_____
honey	_____
delay	_____
away	_____

1 Some verbs do not add **ed** to show the past tense. The spelling changes. Use list words to complete the table.

verb	past tense
	grew
	threw
find	

2 Complete the table by writing each verb in the past tense.

verb	past tense
know	
show	
draw	
chew	

3 Make a new word by changing one letter in each list word. The clues give the meaning of the new word.

list word	new word	clue
mountain	_____	water spouting
delay	_____	a team race
away	_____	move gently from side to side
grow	_____	a large, black bird
ground	_____	surrounding, round about

4 Fill in the missing letters to name three animals.

d _ _ key   m _ _ k _ _   t _ _ k _ _

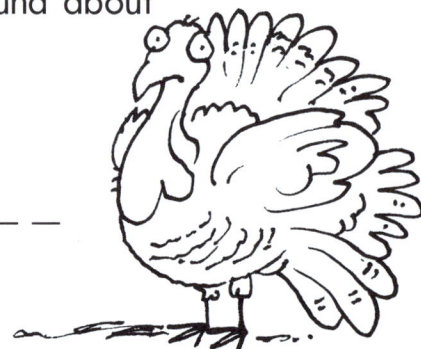

5 👁 Unjumble these letters. The words are all days of the week.

difray _____   dratyusa _____

saddenwey _____   trayshud _____

manyod _____   yestuda _____

Which day haven't you used? _____

6 ✏ Complete each sentence using yester**ay**, tod**ay** or tomorr**ow**.

We will begin our holidays _____.

_____ I rode my bike to the pool.

It is Peter's birthday _____. He is nine.

7 👂 Fill in the missing letters to make rhyming words.

_ _ower   _ _ower   _ ower

_ _own   _ _own   _ _own

8 👁 Proofread this diary entry. There are five mistakes. Circle the mistakes. Write the words correctly at the end.

Today Mum and I found a strey dog. The tag on his collar said he was called Honey. I made a poster and stuck it on our fence. I tied a rop to Honey's collar and we walked around the block. First he rolled on the ground. Then he tried to run a way. Mum's phone rang. It was Honey's owner. When she collected him she offered me some mony but I refused. We all enjoyd seeing Honey jump up to greet his owner.

_____ _____ _____ _____ _____

Cows can fall **asleep** standing up.

Say Listen Look Understand Remember Practise

across _____

always _____

about _____

around _____

almost _____

already _____

ahead _____

asleep _____

above _____

another _____

along _____

altogether _____

1 Write a list word that means the opposite.

behind _____

below _____

separately _____

never _____

awake _____

2 Colour the circle if the **a** at the beginning has a short sound.

alive ◯   after ◯

again ◯   along ◯

almost ◯   away ◯

across ◯   alike ◯

always ◯   aloud ◯

Tip! A **prefix** is a syllable added at the beginning of a word to change the meaning. **un** and **dis** both give the word an opposite meaning.

kind → unkind   approve → disapprove

3 Add **un** or **dis** at the beginning to make a word with the opposite meaning.

_____ happy   _____ safe   _____ obey

_____ agree   _____ tidy   _____ like

4 Write your own words beginning with **un** or **dis**.

un _____   un _____   dis _____

5 Arrange these words from least often to most often.

sometimes   always   often   never   rarely

_____

6 Write list words.

This pen doesn't work. Can you pass me _____ one?

We started our sport lesson by running _____ the yard.

Hurry up! It's _____ two o'clock.

My cat can walk _____ the top of the fence.

We rowed _____ the river for a picnic.

> ⭐ **Tip!** *A long path* is not the same as *along the path*.
> Remember to leave a space between each word in a sentence.

7 Write these sentences leaving spaces between each word.

Donotbeafraid. _____

Mysisterisawaysicktoday. _____

Jackisaloneinthehouse. _____

8 Write your own beginning for a fairy tale. Use as many list words as you can.

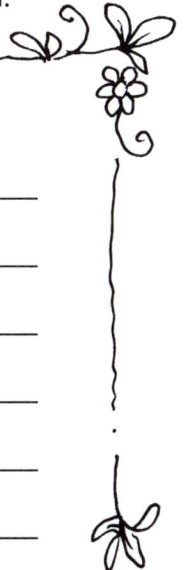

Once upon a time _____

_____

_____

_____

_____

_____

Some leeches can suck out ten times their own weight in human blood.

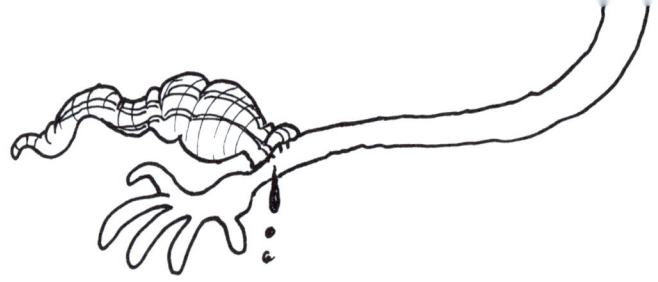

1 Say each word out loud. Change the short vowel to a long vowel by adding **e**.

pip _____   slid _____   fin _____

rob _____   bath _____   mad _____

2 Colour the correct word.

My pyjamas have red and white | strips | stripes |.

We wrote the shopping list on a | scrap | scrape | of paper.

Do you like playing | hid | hide | and seek?

"I need to buy a | tub | tube | of toothpaste," said Brian.

3 In each sentence the underlined word is a noun.
Write your own sentence using the same word as a verb.

Noun: I have a <u>fear</u> of flying.

Verb: _____

Noun: Which <u>rides</u> did you go on at the fair?

Verb: _____

Noun: The <u>waves</u> are crashing onto the rocks.

Verb: _____

4 Colour the correct form of the verb.

I | hope | hoped | the test wouldn't be hard, but it was!

Sam | did | done | his homework before playing soccer.

Kelly | loves | loved | going to the movies when it is raining.

It was Mum's birthday, so I | make | made | her a cake.

5 👁 Write **ee** or **ea** to complete these words.

p _ _ ch   str _ _ t   scr _ _ m   cl _ _ n   sl _ _ p
tr _ _   dr _ _ m   j _ _ ns   fr _ _   _ _ t

6 👁 Write **oa** or **ow** to complete these words.

gr _ _   fl _ _ ted   bel _ _   sh _ _ ed   l _ _ d
kn _ _   pill _ _   f _ _ m   wind _ _   sl _ _

7 👁 Write **ou** or **ow** to complete these words.

sh _ _ t   cl _ _ n   fr _ _ n   c _ _ nt   f _ _ nd
br _ _ n   pr _ _ d   r _ _ nd   dr _ _ ned   cr _ _ n

8 ✏ Choose a word to fit each space.

> above   another   across   around   almost

Tim's best friend is Sandra, who lives _____ the road. They play together

_____ every day. Last weekend they went to the park to play rounders.

Sandra kept hitting the ball high _____ Tim's head. He had to run a long

way after it. Tim asked his older brother Toby to be fielder so he wouldn't have to

keep running _____ after the ball. Sandra hit the next ball high in the air

and Toby caught it!

"Give me _____ chance, will you?" asked Sandra.

The boys laughed and said it was now her turn to get some exercise.

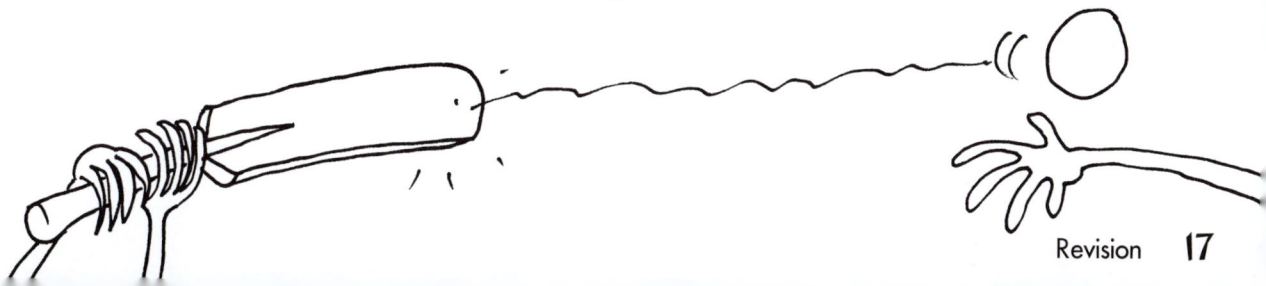

Most people can't keep their eyes open while snee**zing**.

Ah choo

Say Listen Look Understand Remember Practise
shout**ing** _____
bak**ing** _____
beginn**ing** _____
empty**ing** _____
bump**ed** _____
scream**ed** _____
dropp**ed** _____
invit**ed** _____
worri**ed** _____
cross**ly** _____
happi**ly** _____
love**ly** _____

1 Follow the pattern.

jump**s**	jump**ed**	jump**ing**
slurps	_____	_____
shouts	_____	_____

2 Follow the pattern by doubling the consonant.

fit	fitt**ed**	fitt**ing**
skid	_____	_____
trip	_____	_____

3 Follow the pattern by dropping the silent **e**.

race	rac**ed**	rac**ing**
bake	_____	_____
decide	_____	_____

4 Follow the pattern by changing **y** to **i** before adding **es** or **ed**.

try	tr**ies**	tr**ied**	try**ing**
empty	_____	_____	_____
hurry	_____	_____	_____

5 Find a list word to match each rule. Write it in the space.

To make the past tense, if a word ends in:

- two consonants, just add **ed**. _____
- two vowels and a consonant, just add **ed**. _____
- a short vowel and a consonant, double the consonant before adding **ed**. _____
- silent **e**, drop the **e** before adding **ed**. _____
- **y**, change **y** to **i** before adding **ed**. _____

6 Complete each sentence using the correct form of the word in brackets.

I _____ the bucket and stood it upside down. (empty)

Anna lived on a farm before she _____ to town. (move)

Look out! You are _____ everything on the ground. (drop)

Uncle Max is _____ me to the cinema on Saturday. (take)

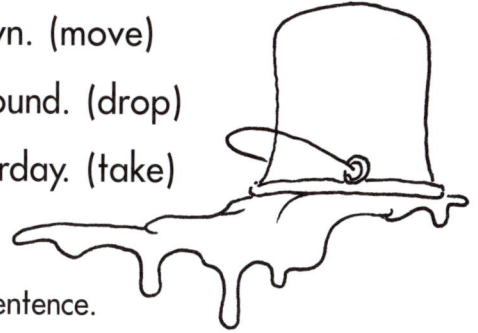

7 Add **ly** to these words. Choose one to complete each sentence.

| loud | cross | love | kind | happy |

"Not stew again!" groaned Peter _____.

"I'd love to come," replied Liam _____.

"Look over here," called Dad _____.

"Can I help you?" asked the shopkeeper _____.

"What a _____ day!" cried Eva as she stepped outside.

8 Find a word that shows how a cook prepares these foods.
It should rhyme with the word in brackets.

_____ water   (spoils)   _____ eggs   (dries)

_____ bread   (shakes)   _____ potatoes (bashes)

_____ sausages (drills)   _____ chicken   (toasts)

9 The spellchecker on my computer says these words are wrong. Actually it is the spaces that are in the wrong places. Write each sentence correctly.

Itwa sbeg in ningtor ain sowea te lun chin theh all.

_____

Samco pied hiss tory neat lyint ohisb ook.

_____

An elephant's trunk has more than 40,000 muscles — more than in a human's whole body!

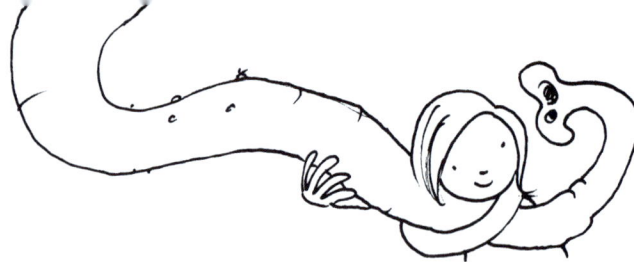

Say Listen Look Understand Remember Practise
Ireland _____
county _____
Belfast _____
Dublin _____
Donegal _____
Cork _____
Galway _____
Kildare _____
Limerick _____
Meath _____
Tipperary _____
Sligo _____
my county

1 Which words are proper nouns? Circle the words that should be written as capitals.

land   harry potter   sea   school

antrim   mr kennedy   michelle

book   david   hospital   fox

2 Write in full:

your name _____

your address _____

_____

3 You have written a letter to your school principal. Follow the example and address the envelope correctly.

Mr R. Smith
Townsville National School
Church Street
Townsville
Co. Kerry

55¢

_____

_____

_____

_____

4 Fill in the missing letters of these county names. The counties may/may not be in your list words.

Ti _ _ er _ ry

_ on _ gh _ _

R _ sc _ _ m _ _

Fe _ ma _ _ gh

D _ n _ g _ _

K _ lk _ _ ny

_ ff _ l _

_ _ xf _ _ _ _

5 👁 Join each county name to the province it belongs to:

Limerick	Leinster	Leitrim	Ulster
Louth	Munster	Tyrone	Connaught
Derry	Ulster	Waterford	Leinster
Sligo	Connaught	Laois	Munster

6 ✏ The days of the week are all proper nouns. Write the days in order.

_____ was the day of the moon.

_____ was Tiw's day. Tiw was the Norse god of war.

_____ was Woden's day. Woden was the chief Norse god.

_____ was Thor's day. Thor was the Norse god of thunder.

_____ was Frigga's day. Frigga was the chief Norse goddess.

_____ was Saturn's day. Saturn was the Roman god of farming.

_____ was the day of the sun.

⭐ **Rule!** **Apostrophes** can show that someone owns something.
Tim's bag.

7 ✍ Use an apostrophe to show who owns each object.

The book belongs to Rachel. It is _____.

The coat belongs to Kieran. It is _____.

The shoes belong to Stacey. They are _____.

The scarf belongs to Mum. It is _____.

8 👁 Circle the letters that should be written as capitals.

the irish sea separates ireland and britain.

shauna goes to limerick for rugby training every friday.

The sperm whale holds the record for the bigg**est** brain. It weighs about 7 or 8 kg.

Encyclopedia

Say Listen Look Understand Remember Practise	
bigg**er**	_____
hott**er**	_____
nic**er**	_____
clos**er**	_____
high**er**	_____
larg**er**	_____
happi**er**	_____
cheap**est**	_____
fast**est**	_____
loud**est**	_____
fitt**est**	_____
funni**est**	_____

1 👁 Follow the patterns.

long	longer	longest
loud	_____	_____
hard	_____	_____
fat	fatter	fattest
big	_____	_____
thin	_____	_____
wide	wider	widest
close	_____	_____
large	_____	_____
funny	funnier	funniest
happy	_____	_____
dirty	_____	_____

⭐ **Tip!** Some **adjectives** change when you use them to compare different things.
good → better → best   bad → worse → worst

2 💭 Choose the word that fits each sentence.

I am good at high jump but I'm _____ at long jump.

I am bad at breast stroke but I'm _____ at backstroke.

Osman sang a solo at the concert as he is the _____ singer in our class.

I don't like it when my sister makes dinner. She is the _____ cook I know.

3 ✏ The adjective *nice* is used too often. Find a better word for each sentence.

My cousin is very nice. _____

This cake is nice. _____

4 ✏️ The blend **st** can begin or end words. Write your own words with **st**.

st _____ _____ _____ _____

_____ st _____ _____ _____ _____

5 🖐️ Use a form of the word in brackets to complete each sentence.

We moved house and now I live much _____ to my school. (close)

Mt Everest is the _____ mountain in the world. (high)

Kyle is the _____ boy in our class. (tall)

If you go to football training you will get _____ . (fit)

6 👁️ Use your dictionary!

Find a compound word that begins with **story**. _____

What is the next word after **stork**? _____

What is the word before **toast**? _____

What is the guide word written on the top of the page where you find the word

stretch? _____

Write the dictionary meaning for **coast**: _____

_____

Arrange in alphabetical order: strong, stale, stink, stupid, stage

_____ _____ _____ _____ _____

7 👁️ The errors in this passage are all homophones.
Circle each one and write the correct form of the word.

Last night we had stake for dinner. _____

I couldn't finish my peace so I gave _____

it to our dog. Dad said that was a _____

waist because their is never enough _____

meet on his plate! _____

People used to believe the Earth was flat, and that if you walked far enough you'd fall off!

Say Listen Look Understand Remember Practise
brief _____
grief _____
relief _____
fielder _____
fierce _____
shield _____
niece _____
piece _____
sieve _____
thieve _____
believe _____
friend _____

1 Find a list word that rhymes.

leaf _____

peeled _____

crease _____

live _____

mend _____

beef _____

2 Write a list word for each clue.

not long _____

the daughter of your brother or sister _____

a container with holes _____

sadness _____

steal _____

3 Make a list word by changing one letter in each word.

pierce _____

relieve _____

grief _____

niece _____

4 Follow the example to complete the table.

noun	verb	sentence (using either word)
grief	grieve	My neighbour cried with grief when his dog died.
	relieve	
belief		

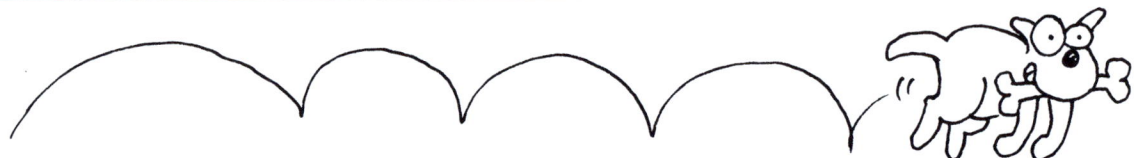

24 Digraph ie; homophones piece/peace, cheap/cheep

5 🖍 Use the clues to complete the words.

a caterpillar's favourite food

the top of a house

the person in charge

meat from a cow

not able to hear

bread is baked in this shape

$1 \div 2 =$

a game played with a club

a flat surface to put things on

a dangerous hunting animal

		E		F
	R			F
		I		F
			E	F
	D			F
	L			F
			L	F
	G			F
		E		F
	W			F

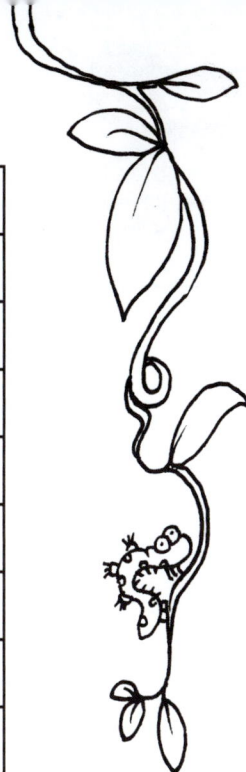

⭐ **Tip!**

Learn these homophones:

piece = a part   **cheap** = not expensive

peace = not at war   **cheep** = sound of a bird

---

6 👁 Colour the correct word.

May I have another | piece | peace | of cake?

Everyone wants to live in | piece | peace |.

The chicks | cheap | cheep | noisily when they are hungry.

Theatre tickets are | cheap | cheep | on Tuesdays.

---

7 💭 Find a list word that belongs to each group.

mate   buddy   _____   loss   sadness   _____

sword   helmet   _____   cousin nephew   _____

steal   burgle   _____   scary   wild   _____

---

8 🖍 Write one sentence using both words.

friend	_____
piece	_____

When you sneeze, air and snot fly out of your nose at 160 km/h. **Dis**gusting!

Say Listen Look Understand Remember Practise

untidy _____

unlikely _____

mischief _____

misplace _____

misbehave _____

mistake _____

disagree _____

disgrace _____

disgusting _____

dishonest _____

disobey _____

discover _____

1 Make a word that means the opposite by adding **un**, **mis** or **dis** at the beginning.

_____lucky   _____agree

_____behave   _____safe

_____healthy   _____honest

_____appear   _____understand

_____obey   _____tidy

_____place   _____true

_____likely   _____like

2 Give each sentence the opposite meaning by adding **un**, **mis**, or **dis**.

The sun appeared over the horizon.

_____

Your desk is so tidy!

_____

Sam really likes Irish dancing.

_____

I agree with you.

_____

The train is likely to arrive on time.

_____

Synonyms are words with the same meaning. *Small* and *little* are synonyms.

3 🗣️ Find list words that are synonyms for these words.

error _____   find _____

lose _____   messy _____

gross _____   act badly _____

4 👂 Jason's bedroom is a mess. Describe each object using an adjective that rhymes with the clue. Then say where each object is in his room. Finally, draw the bedroom to match your sentences.

Jason's <u>shiny</u> bike helmet is <u>on the floor.</u> How untidy!
     (tiny)

His _____ socks are _____. How disgusting!
  (jelly)

His _____ football is _____. What a disgrace!
  (thirty)

His _____ jacket is _____. How unlikely!
  (blue)

5 ✏️ Use your dictionary to find the meaning of these words. Use both words in one sentence.

| dismay | _____ |
| mishap | _____ |

It is **im**possible to lick your own elbow!

1 Complete the tables.

word	add er	add est
big		
wide		
quiet		
pretty		

word	add ly
quick	
safe	
friend	
happy	

word	add ed	add ing
smile		
groan		
drop		
worry		

word	add y
wind	
health	
dream	
mess	

2 Make a new word by adding a prefix from the box.

un	dis	mis	re

_____turn   _____tidy   _____take   _____cover

_____agree   _____behave   _____likely   _____arrange

3 Fill in the missing vowels.

bel _ _ ve   disapp _ _ nt   fr _ _ nd   disapp _ _ r

disagr _ _   misch _ _ f   qu _ _ tly   f _ _ rce

empt _ _ d   l _ _ dly   p _ _ ceful   m _ _ nt _ _ n

4 Fill in the seven days of the week.

5 Circle the letters that should be written as capitals. Add the missing punctuation.

my name is james and i am afraid of spiders. like most homes i know there are plenty of spiders in my house.

last sunday i was sitting at home reading harry potter and the deathly hallows by j k rowling. mum called me and i looked up. there it was. a huge spider. mum isnt afraid of spiders at all. she picked it up and popped it in to my brothers gym bag. i breathed again.

6 Add a letter to the beginning of each word to make a new word.

_ lean	_ nail	_ rail	_ tone	_ room
_ rain	_ lower	_ new	_ now	_ rush
_ heat	_ harm	_ rack	_ rust	_ lack

In France, children leave a pair of shoes out to be filled with presents at Christmas time.

Say Listen Look Understand Remember Practise

Christmas _____

angel _____

shepherd _____

donkey _____

manger _____

carol _____

holly _____

wreath _____

present _____

stocking _____

reindeer _____

celebrate _____

1 Make words using letters from these list words.

wreath _____ _____

angel _____ _____

present _____ _____

celebrate _____ _____

manger _____ _____

stocking _____ _____

_____ _____ _____

Christmas

_____ _____ _____

2 Complete the table.

singular	plural
wish	
wreath	
reindeer	
donkey	
elf	
party	

3 Add **ion** to make nouns.

verb	noun
celebrate	
decorate	
act	
reject	
instruct	
direct	

4 ✏️ Sort the words into categories.

| wreath | candle | holly | pudding | tinsel |
| ham | wrap | stocking | turkey | Santa |

decorations	presents	food

5 🔊 Colour the correct word.

Silent night, [holly | holy] night

Away in a [manager | manger], no crib for a bed

Hark! the herald [angels | angles] sing!

The [holly | holy] and the ivy

6 ✏️ Write Santa's reply to Sarah's letter.

Dear Santa,

My Mum says no one thinks to give you a present. Is that true? What would you like for Christmas?

Love, Sarah

_____

_____

_____

_____

_____

_____

_____

_____

Meerkats are very help**ful** animals. They often take care of each other's babies.

Say Listen Look Understand Remember Practise
joy**ful** _____
use**ful** _____
play**ful** _____
cheer**ful** _____
help**ful** _____
aw**ful** _____
care**ful** _____
pain**ful** _____
peace**ful** _____
colour**ful** _____
grate**ful** _____
beaut**iful** _____

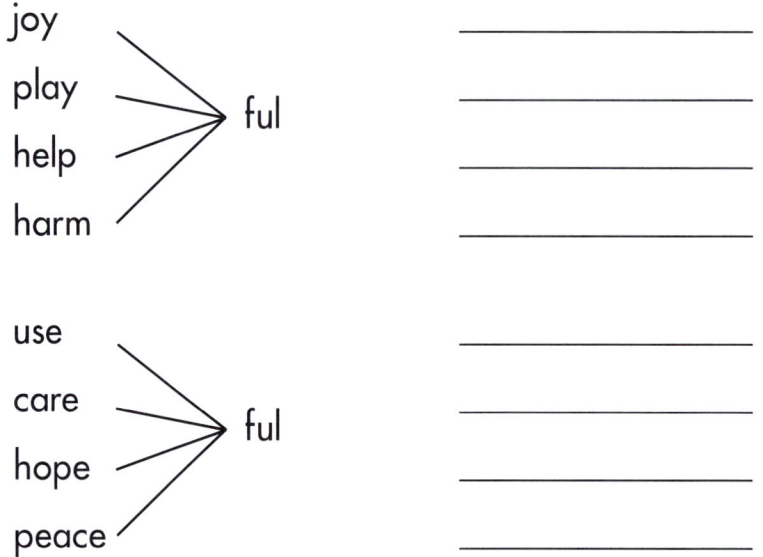

1 Add **ful** to these words.

joy
play
help
harm
⟩ **ful**

_____
_____
_____
_____

use
care
hope
peace
⟩ **ful**

_____
_____
_____
_____

Rule! If a word ends in **y**, change **y** to **i** before adding **ful**.
beauty → beautiful

2 Add **ful** to these words.

duty → _____

mercy → _____

pity → _____

plenty → _____

3 Words for quantities sometimes end in **ful**. *Handful* is an example. Use the pictures as clues to write these quantities.

_____

_____

_____

_____

_____

_____

4 ✏️ Use the clue to find a list word to fit each sentence.

My nickname is Smiley as I am always _____. (in a good mood)

Our classroom is bright and _____. (has many colours)

"Thank you! I am _____ you could help." (thankful)

A sprained ankle can be very _____. (sore)

Did you see the _____ sunrise this morning? (pretty)

⭐ **Tip!**

A **mnemonic** is a trick to help us remember something.
Peace and *piece* are homophones.
The mnemonic *I'd like a piece of pie* can help you remember the difference.

---

5 💭 Think up your own mnemonics for these words.

grateful _____

beautiful _____

colourful _____

6 👁️ Change only one letter at a time to make the new word.

H	A	N	D
C	A	R	E

S	O	N
B	U	Y

S	T	A	R	E
S	H	O	R	T

7 ✏️ Write your own sentences using these words.

awful
wonderful

_____

_____

Unit 15

Funnel web spider venom is harm**less** to dogs and cats.

Say Listen Look Understand Remember Practise
less _____
hope**less** _____
harm**less** _____
heart**less** _____
fear**less** _____
pre**ss** _____
gra**ss** _____
gue**ss** _____
expre**ss** _____
progre**ss** _____
compa**ss** _____
prince**ss** _____

1 Add **less** to these words.

harm
heart } **less** _____
fear   _____
worth   _____
            _____

use
hope } **less** _____
care   _____
shape   _____
            _____

⭐ **Rule!** If a word ends in **y**, change **y** to **i** before adding **less**.

2 Add **less** to these words.

pity _____   mercy _____

3 Complete the table by writing the word if it makes sense.
If you can't make a sensible word, put a cross.

base word	add ful	add less
use		
play		
care		
fear		

4 👁 Colour the correct word.

The brave hero was | fearless | harmless | as he fought the dragon.

A woman who marries a prince becomes a | priceless | princess |.

Cows need to eat plenty of | grass | glass |.

"You'll never | guest | guess | what happened to me today!"

5 👁 Write **s** or **ss** to complete each word.

alway____   expre____   acro____

progre____   almo____t   pre____ing

cla____room   dre____ed   unle____

6 ✏ Write the names of the four points of the compass.

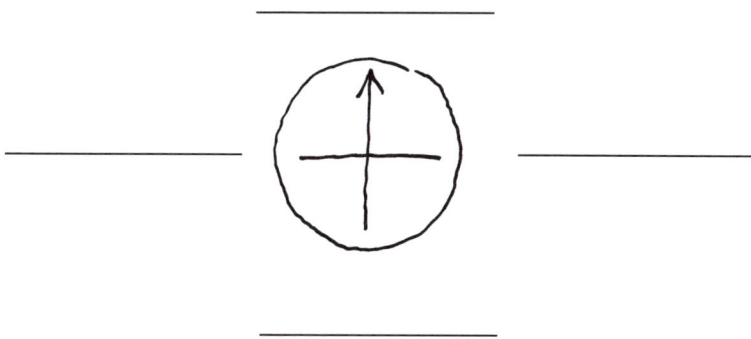

_____

_____   _____

_____

north
south
east
west

Tip! ⭐ *Guessed* and *guest* are **homophones**.
Guessed is a verb and *guest* is a noun.

7 👁 If a word is a homophone, a computer's spellchecker will not notice a mistake.
Circle the errors in these sentences and correct them.

Are you shore you can eat a hole apple? _____ _____

I rowed my bike too kilometres. _____ _____

Dad said to leave our guessed in piece. _____ _____

When a horse gallops, all four hooves are off the ground at once.

Say Listen Look Understand Remember Practise
letter _____
butter _____
gallop _____
balloon _____
kennel _____
tunnel _____
tennis _____
rubbish _____
summer _____
lesson _____
blossom _____
burrow _____

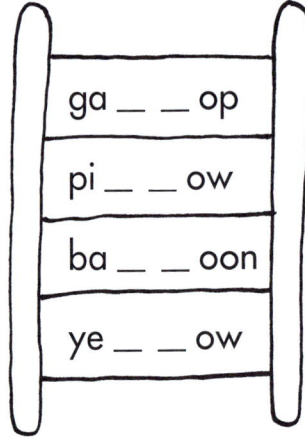

1 The words in each ladder are missing the same double letters. Write the missing letters.

ga _ _ op
pi _ _ ow
ba _ _ oon
ye _ _ ow

rr
ss
tt
nn
ll

ke _ _ el
di _ _ er
tu _ _ el
wi _ _ er

le _ _ on
blo _ _ om

bu _ _ ow
so _ _ ow

le _ _ er
bu _ _ er
ki _ _ en

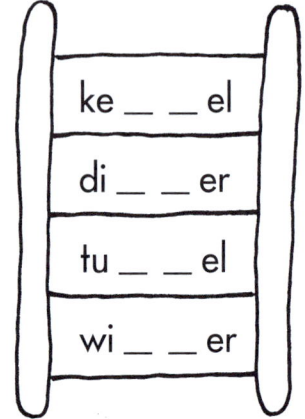

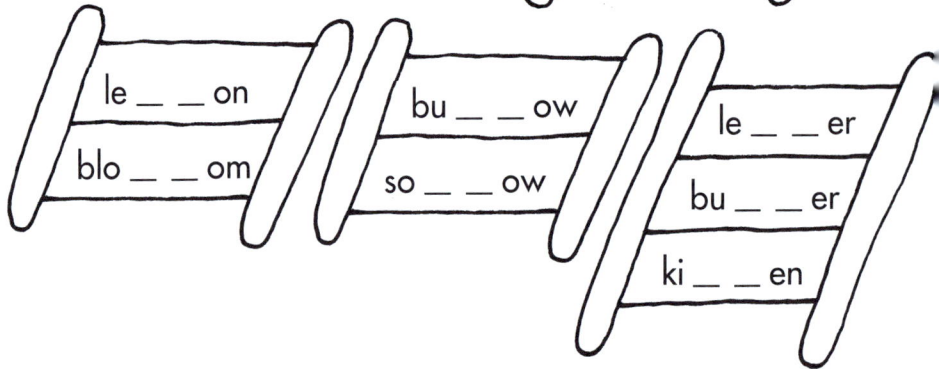

2 Use the clue to complete each word.

_ _ rr _ _   a colourful bird

_ _ rr _ _   a long orange vegetable

_ _ rr _ _   an animal's underground home

_ _ mm _ _   a tool for hitting nails

_ _ mm _ _   a warm season

_ _ dd _ _   useful for reaching high places

_ _ bb _ _   used for making car tyres

_ _ bb _ _ _   litter

_ _ _ pp _ _   a warm shoe to wear indoors

3 ✏️ Change one letter in the underlined word to make a new word.
Use the new word in your own sentence.

Let the soup <u>simmer</u> for one hour.

_____

The green apple tasted <u>bitter</u>.

_____

Hardly any words start with the <u>letter</u> x.

_____

My dog likes to have a ride in the <u>barrow</u>.

_____

4 🖐️ Choose one word from each box to make compound words.

letter	wheel	grass	button	pillow
hopper	box	hole	case	barrow

_____   _____   _____

_____   _____

5 👁️ Circle the words that need double letters and write them correctly.

We never leave rubish in our back garden. But   _____ _____

last night my dog, Oscar, knocked over the bin   _____ _____

and the lid came of. A seagul colected some   _____ _____

stale bread and ate it for diner. Then it caried a   _____ _____

plastic bag up to the roof. Dad used a lader   _____ _____

to climb up and get it back. I tied Oscar to his

kenel as he was trying to burow under the fence.   _____

He quickly sliped out of his colar and ran away.

What a night!

The first bubble gum was made in ancient Greece from tree resin.

Say Listen Look Understand Remember Practise

apple _____

saddle _____

puddle _____

riddle _____

cuddle _____

bubble _____

bottle _____

kettle _____

little _____

juggle _____

giggle _____

wriggle _____

1 Write the double letters.

pp   dd   bb   tt   gg

pu _ _ le   ke _ _ le

wri _ _ le   sa _ _ le

cu _ _ le   a _ _ le

bu _ _ le   gi _ _ le

bo _ _ le   ri _ _ le

li _ _ le   ju _ _ le

2 Change one letter to make a new word.

riddle (m) _____   juggle (str) _____

puddle (a) _____   bottle (a) _____

giggle (j) _____   middle (f) _____

3 Make new words by adding **le** to these words.

buck _____   tick _____

pick _____   crack _____

chuck _____   tack _____

> **Tip!**
> The **k** in **kn** is a silent letter. *knuckle*
> The **w** in **wr** is a silent letter. *wriggle*

4 👁 Fill in the missing silent letter. Choose **k** or **w**.

_ nee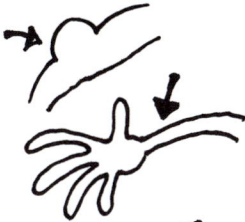

_ nuckle

_ rite

_ rist

_ rong   1 + 1 = 3 ✗

_ not

_ nife

_ nit

_ riggle

5 Here are some interesting words to use instead of *talk*. Write the words in the correct speech bubble.

jabber	bellow	mutter	shout
whisper	gabble	roar	mumble
shriek	murmur	babble	chatter

talk quietly
_____   _____
_____   _____

talk loudly
_____   _____
_____   _____

talk quickly
_____
_____
_____

6 👁 Use your dictionary to find a word beginning with **fra** to match each meaning.

fra _ _ _ _ _ _   a break in a bone

fra _ _ _ _ _   easily broken

fra _ _ _ _ _ _   a small, broken piece of something

fra _ _ _ _ _ _   having a pleasant smell

fra _ _ _ _ _ _ _   a tree with large yellow and white flowers

The Roman emperor, Julius Caesar, named the month of July after himself.

Say Listen Look Understand Remember Practise

January _____

February _____

March _____

April _____

May _____

June _____

July _____

August _____

September _____

October _____

November _____

December _____

1 Unjumble the letters for each month. Don't forget to start with a capital letter!

luyj

_____

bemveron

_____

tugusa

_____

recembed

_____

enju

_____

perbmeets

_____

jurayan

_____

aym

_____

fryubare

_____

charm

_____

brotoce

_____

prail

_____

2 How many days are there in each month? Use the number clues to complete this rhyme.

Clue: January = 1   December = 12

Thirty days have _____ , _____ , _____
                          9   4   6

and _____ .
         11

All the rest have thirty-one,

Except for _____ alone
                    2

Which has twenty-eight days clear

And twenty-nine in each leap year!

3 ✏️ Write the months that match each season. Which is your favourite month? Why?

summer	autumn	winter	spring
_____	_____	_____	_____
_____	_____	_____	_____
_____	_____	_____	_____

My favourite month is _____

_____

⭐ **Tip!** **Proper nouns** name people, places, pets, days of the week, months, books and poems. Proper nouns are always written with a capital letter.

4 👁️ Circle the nouns that need capital letters in these sentences.

My uncle josh is driving his motorbike from cork to donegal in july.

It was my birthday last friday and grandad gave me a book about roy keane.

5 ✏️ Write a sentence using as many proper nouns as you can that begin with the same letter.

Jennifer Jones, who was born in January, lives in Julianstown.

_____

_____

6 💭 Complete the table to build word families.

noun	adjective	compound word or noun group
	daily	daytime
week		
		lunar month
		leap year

The bigg**est** frog in the world is the Goliath frog. A Goliath frog can weigh as much as a house cat!

1 These words all have one or two prefixes or suffixes. Write the base words to which the prefixes and suffixes were added.

unhelpful _____   littlest _____   burrowed _____

awfully _____   guessing _____   disappear _____

returned _____   bravely _____   replied _____

beginning _____   pitiless _____   beautiful _____

2 Add the prefix or suffix shown to each base word.

empty + ed _____   pain + ful + ly _____

juggle + ing _____   pretty + est _____

hope + less _____   mis + understand _____

worry + ed _____   fear + ful _____

Rule! Two-syllable words with a double consonant break into syllables between the consonants.

puddle = pud/dle   tennis = ten/nis   butter = but/ter

3 Mark the syllable breaks in these words. In the circle, write the number of syllables you hear.

January ◯   April ◯   July ◯

giggle ◯   wriggled ◯   apples ◯

balloon ◯   rubbish ◯   bubbling ◯

playfully ◯   colourful ◯   summer ◯

Antonyms are words with the opposite meaning.
Big and *little* are antonyms.
Antonyms are also formed using prefixes and suffixes.
kind **un**kind   harm**ful** harm**less**

4 Write an antonym for each of these words.

hard _____   long _____   hopeless _____

tidy _____   end _____   painful _____

5 Where does each animal live?

dog _____   horse _____   fox _____

rabbit _____   bird _____   pig _____

goldfish _____   bee _____   owl _____

6 Make a new word by adding a consonant at the beginning.

_ tale   _ each   _ our   _ harp   _ ear

_ nail   _ port   _ lame   _ lean   _ are

7 Make a new word by adding a letter at the end.

ski _   she _   rid _   was _   pea _

not _   dam _   grin _   bat _   win _

8 Make a new word by adding an extra vowel in the middle.

pin _____   man _____   shut _____

bat _____   flat _____   rod _____

Your w**eigh**t on the moon is six times less than your weight on Earth.

Say Listen Look Understand Remember Practise

s**igh** _____

s**igh**t _____

m**igh**t _____

br**igh**t _____

midn**igh**t _____

fr**igh**ten _____

kn**igh**t _____

eight _____

n**eigh** _____

w**eigh**t _____

sl**eigh** _____

n**eigh**bour _____

1 How many words can you make with **ight**?

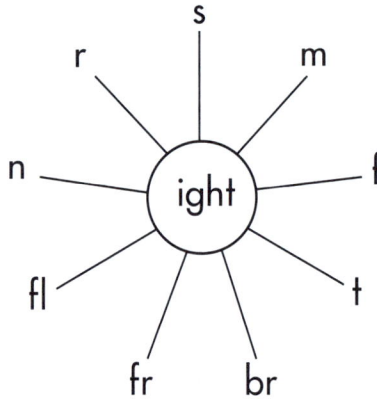

s

r   m

n   **ight**   f

fl   t

fr   br

_____   _____

_____

_____

_____

_____

_____

_____

2 Make words ending in **igh**.

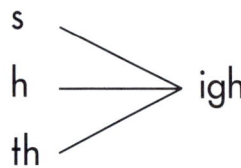

s

h ————— **igh**

th

_____

_____

_____

3 Choose one syllable from each box to make a word with two syllables.

to	de	neigh
twi	mid	high
in	al	light

night	sight	house
light	bour	ready

_____   _____   _____

_____   _____   _____

_____   _____   _____

4 Complete the tables.

noun	verb
	see
weight	

noun	verb
	fly
fright	

5 Is the circled word a noun or a verb?

The horse (neighed) loudly as I approached. _____

The first visitors to the South Pole used (sleighs) pulled by husky dogs. _____

It's time to (light) the barbecue for lunch. _____

6 Write a sentence using each word.

smell (noun) _____

smell (verb) _____

sigh (noun) _____

sigh (verb) _____

7 Write a list word for each category.

time _____   number _____   person _____

8 Colour the correct homophone.

Do | nights | knights | take their armour off at | night | knight | ?

In English we | right | write | our words from left to | right | write | .

Gorillas can be **taught** to use sign language to communicate with people.

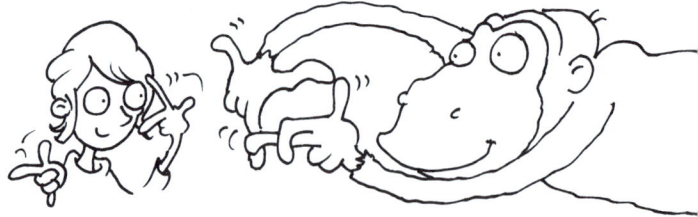

Say Listen Look Understand Remember Practise	
t**ough**	_____
r**ough**	_____
c**ough**	_____
en**ough**	_____
th**ough**	_____
th**ough**t	_____
b**ough**t	_____
f**ough**t	_____
t**aught**	_____
c**aught**	_____
d**augh**ter	_____
n**augh**ty	_____

1 Write **ou** or **au**.

c _ _ gh   t _ _ ght

c _ _ ght   th _ _ gh

en _ _ gh   r _ _ gh

d _ _ ghter   b _ _ ght

t _ _ gh   n _ _ ghty

★ **Rule!** Most verbs show the past tense by adding **ed**.

discover → discovered

Some verbs have a different form in the past tense.

write → wrote

2 Complete the tables.

verb	past tense
buy	
cough	
teach	

verb	past tense
think	
fight	
weigh	

3 Choose the right word for each space.

tough	though	through	thought

The piece of steak was too _____ to chew.

Even _____ it was sunny, I _____ it might rain later.

The lion jumped _____ the burning hoop.

Antonyms are words with the opposite meaning.
day, night

4 Write an antonym for each word.

good _____   dropped _____   up _____

under _____   smooth _____   sold _____

5 Find the antonyms by circling the words that don't make sense.
Write the word with the opposite meaning.

_____

_____

_____

_____

_____

It was midday on Christmas Eve. As there was no moon it was very dark. Sam wanted to stay asleep so he could catch Santa Claus delivering presents. He heard a soft crash outside and jumped out of bed to shine his torch through the window. Two dull shiny eyes blinked, then disappeared. It was just a cat. Sam turned around to climb back into bed and gasped. Leaning against his bed was a tiny package. It must be the new bike he wanted. But how had it got there?

6 Write the noun for the family member who is . . .

the daughter of your aunt: your _____

the wife of your grandfather: your _____

the son of your mother: your _____

the daughter of your sister: your _____

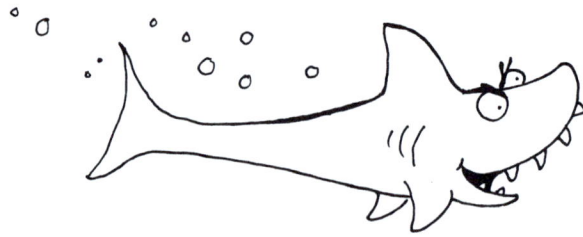

Sharks can't swim back**ward**s.

Say Listen Look Understand Remember Practise
sad**ness** _____
happi**ness** _____
revis**ion** _____
televis**ion** _____
direct**ion** _____
friend**ship** _____
king**dom** _____
free**dom** _____
for**ward** _____
back**ward** _____
child**hood** _____
neighbour**hood**
_____

1 Make nouns by choosing the right suffix to add to these words.

> **ness**   **ship**   **dom**   **hood**

kind_____   friend_____

king_____   late_____

dark_____   loud_____

child_____   truthful_____

sad_____   free_____

neighbour_____   tired_____

forgetful_____   sponsor_____

⭐ **Rule!** If an adjective ends in **y**, change the **y** to **i** before adding **ness**.

lonely → loneliness

2 Add **ness** to these words.

happy   lazy   empty

_____   _____   _____

ugly   friendly   dizzy

_____   _____   _____

3 Which of the nouns on this page might you hear in a fairy tale?

Rule! Some verbs can be changed into nouns by adding **ion**.

If the verb ends in **e**, drop the **e** before adding **ion**.

confuse → *confusion*

4 Complete the tables.

noun	verb
	discuss
separation	
	act
revision	

noun	verb
introduction	
	direct
explanation	
	televise

5 Name each mathematical operation. Each one ends in **ion**.

2 + 3 = 5 _____

6 − 2 = 4 _____

4 x 2 = 8 _____

6 ÷ 3 = 2 _____

6 The suffix **ward** means *in the direction of*. Write three words that use this suffix and give the antonym for each one.

	word	**antonym**
in		
for → ward		
up		

7 Make a noun by adding a suffix to the adjective. Look in a dictionary!
Use each noun in a sentence.

wise	_____
likely	_____

Only female mosquit**oes**
suck blood.

Say Listen Look Understand Remember Practise

t**oe** _____

can**oe** _____

tomat**o** _____

potat**o** _____

mang**o** _____

her**o** _____

pian**o** _____

kangaro**o** _____

dozen _____

women _____

trousers _____

scissors _____

★ Rule!

If a noun ends in **o**, you usually add **es** to make the plural.
  echo ➝ echoes

If the word comes from another language, you usually add **s** to make the plural.
  avocado (Spanish) ➝ avocados
  piano (Italian) ➝ pianos

If the word ends in two vowels, just add **s**.
  radio ➝ radios

1 Write the plural ending for these nouns.

canoe____   mosquito____

hero____   kimono____

radio____   toe____

volcano____   kangaroo____

piano____   video____

banjo____   studio____

2 Write the plural ending for the items on this list.

3 kg potato____

1 kg tomato____

2 mango____

2 avocado____

0.5 kg pea____

4 banana____

3 Why is there no singular form for these words?

scissors   tongs   pliers   trousers   tweezers

Because _____

_____

4 Complete the tables.

singular	plural
woman	
	oxen
sheep	

singular	plural
	deer
goose	
	photos

> ★ **Tip!**
>
> Take care with these homophones.
> **there** = a place (<u>here</u> and <u>there</u>)
> **their** = belonging to them (is always followed by a noun)
> **they're** = they are
> *Where are their clothes? They're over there!*

5 Write your own sentences to show how each word is used.

(there) _____

_____

(their) _____

_____

(they're) _____

_____

6 An abbreviation is a short form of a longer word. Use your dictionary to find the longer word for each abbreviation.

hippo _____   rhino _____

photo _____   kilo _____

No two giraffes have the same pattern on their skin.

Say Listen Look Understand Remember Practise	
puff	_____
cliff	_____
staff	_____
shelf	_____
half	_____
wolf	_____
scarf	_____
leaf	_____
knife	_____
themselves	_____
handkerchief	_____
giraffe	_____

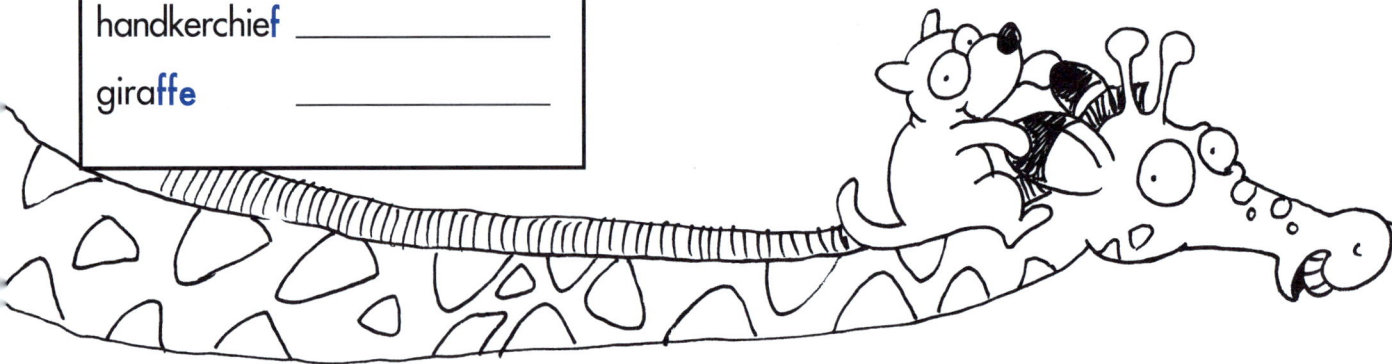

1 Find a list word that rhymes.

calf	laugh	wife
_____	_____	_____
stiff	thief	bluff
_____	_____	_____

2 Write how many syllables each word has.

themselves ◯   shelf ◯

handkerchief ◯   giraffe ◯

Rule! If a noun ends in **f** or **fe**, change the **f** or **fe** to **v** and add **es** to form the plural.

elf → elves   life → lives

If a noun ends in **ff** or **ffe**, add **s** to form the plural.

---

3 Write the plural for each noun.

half _____   loaf _____   knife _____

puff _____   thief _____   cliff _____

yourself _____   shelf _____   giraffe _____

A **collective noun** names a group of people, animals or things.

a pod of whales   *a fleet of ships*   *an army of soldiers*

4 👁 Choose an animal to complete each collective noun. Use a dictionary if you need help.

| wolves | kittens | bees | sheep | cattle | fish |

a flock of _____   a school of _____

a litter of _____   a swarm of _____

a herd of _____   a pack of _____

Write one more collective noun. a _____ of _____

Make up one yourself. a _____ of _____

5 👂 Add a consonant to the beginning of each word to make a new word that rhymes.
ring ⟶ bring

_ lane   _ room   _ rain   _ row   _ pace

_ rust   _ lace   _ low   _ rush   _ win

6 ✏ Write an antonym for each clue.

A		K					
B			L				
C				H			
D					R		
E						T	
F							T
G								Y
H									L

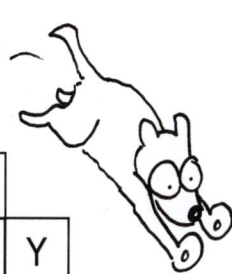

A   answer

B   freeze

C   drop

D   safety

E   hardest

F   closest

G   suddenly

H   vertical

Tomat**oes** are really a kind of fruit, not a vegetable!

1  Fill in the missing vowels.

_ _ ght   w _ _ ght   h _ _ ght   b _ _ ght   c _ _ ght

2 Fill in the missing consonants.

ni _ _ t   nei _ _ _ our   s _ ei _ _   s _ i _ _ or _   _ an _ a _ oo

3 Add suffixes to these adjectives to make adverbs and nouns.

adjective	sad	kind	happy	free	lazy
adverb					
noun					

4 Make a new noun by adding one or two suffixes.

king_____   friend_____   child_____   truth_____

5 Complete the tables.

singular	plural
canoe	
	tomatoes
hero	
	women

singular	plural
cliff	
	shelves
scarf	
	wolves

6 Write the homophone for each word.

pore	site	threw	weight	write
____	____	____	____	____

bolder	choose	wade	allowed	stares
____	____	____	____	____

7 Circle the words which are not used correctly in this story.

Last holidays we flew on a plain to France. The flight took too hours and I had red most of my book by the time we landed. I couldn't sleep because there was a noisy baby only too rose behind us. She didn't give her parents a moment of piece the hole journey.

The whether was hot and sticky every day, so Mum decided we should all by some knew summer clothes. When we packed to go home our suitcase was so full I thought it might brake.

⭐ **Tip!** An **anagram** is formed by rearranging the letters in a word.
Lemon is an anagram of *melon*.

---

8 Use the clues to make anagrams of these words.

cars _____ a mark on the skin

thorn _____ one of the points on a compass

state _____ one of the five senses

Snakes use their tongues to smell.

Say Listen Look Understand Remember Practise	
wrap	_____
wrinkle	_____
kneel	_____
ca**l**m	_____
cas**t**le	_____
com**b**	_____
i**s**land	_____
honest	_____
tong**ue**	_____
autum**n**	_____
dou**b**t	_____
g**h**ost	_____

1 Circle the silent letter in each of these words. Write a list word with the same silent letter.

palm	hour
_____	_____
debt	listen
_____	_____
wrong	thumb
_____	_____
solemn	knock
_____	_____

2 These body parts all have silent letters. Write the word.

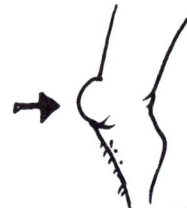

_____   _____   _____

_____   _____   _____

3 Add a suffix to each word.

ghost + ly _____   comb + ing _____

wrap + ed _____   wrinkle + ing _____

doubt + ful _____   honest + y _____

Rule! ⭐ Some letters just don't go together in English. There are also some letters that just can't start or end words.

- **q** is always followed by **u**.
- No English words end with **v**.
- No English words start with **pf**.

4 👁 These words have all come from another language. That is why the spelling looks odd. Match each type of boat to its description. The first one has been done for you.

canoe (Spanish)   a boat with sails

kayak (Inuit)   a very small rowboat

yacht (Dutch)   a light boat with a cover that fits around the paddler's waist

catamaran (Tamil)   a boat with two joined hulls

dinghy (Hindi)   a lightweight boat with paddles

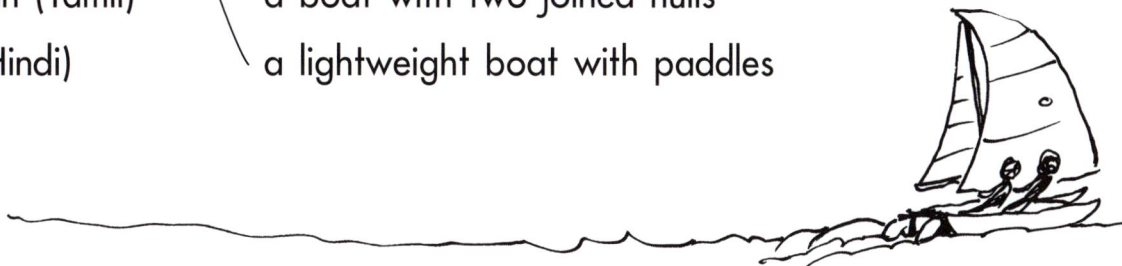

5 ✏ There are many words you can use instead of *went*.
The dog <u>wriggled</u> through the narrow gap in the fence.
Find a better word than *went* to complete these sentences.

The ghost _____ through the door.

The elephant _____ through the reeds to reach the waterhole.

Jack and Jill _____ up the hill to fetch a pail of water.

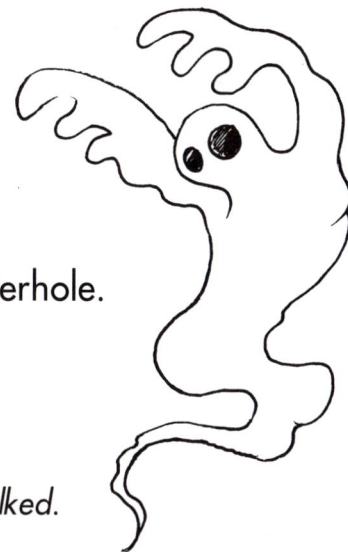

6 ✏ Fill in the missing vowels to make words you can use instead of *walked*.
Use two of these verbs in your own sentences.

str _ d _   d _ wdl _ d   t _ pt _ _ d   w _ ddl _ d   tr _ dg _ d

Dublin is Ireland's largest city. Over one million people live there.

Say Listen Look Understand Remember Practise
carpet _____
cancel _____
cent _____
once _____
city _____
correct _____
cure _____
lettuce _____
cucumber _____
cylinder _____
because _____
decide _____

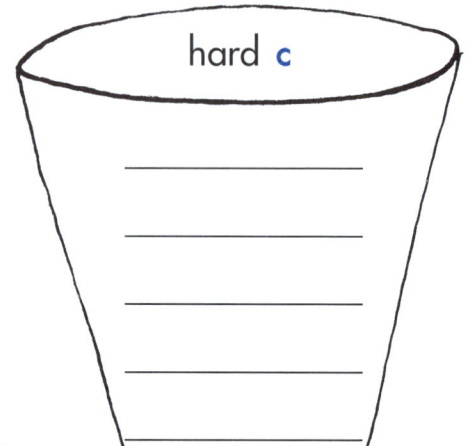

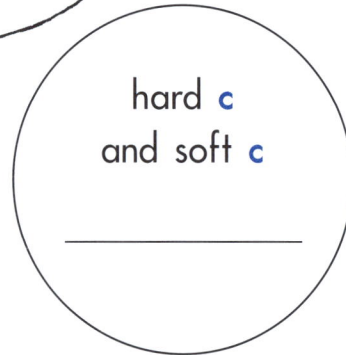

1 Say each list word aloud and listen to the sound the c makes. Write the word inside the appropriate shape.

soft c

_____
_____
_____
_____

hard c

_____
_____
_____
_____
_____

hard c and soft c

_____

2 Look at the letters following c in each group of words in question 1. Fill in the missing letters for the two rules.

c is soft like s when the next letter is _, _ or _.

c is hard like k when the next letter is _, _ or _.

3 Fill in the missing letters for these vegetables. If you need help, use a dictionary.

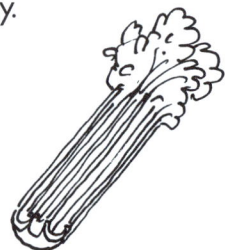

c _ b _ _ g _   c _ _ u _ b _ _   _ e _ t _ c _   _ a _ r _ _   _ el _ r _

4 👁 The missing letters all make an **s** sound. Write **c** or **s**.

_ertain	_illy	_ircle	_ircu_	_urfa_e
_entre	_imple	_ement	_ervice	_eiling

5 👁 The missing letters all make a **k** sound. Write **c** or **k**.

_oala	_urtain	_olour	_ettle	_upboard
_on_rete	_itchen	_orrect	_itten	_rin_le

6 ✏ Complete the crossword puzzle.

Across

3.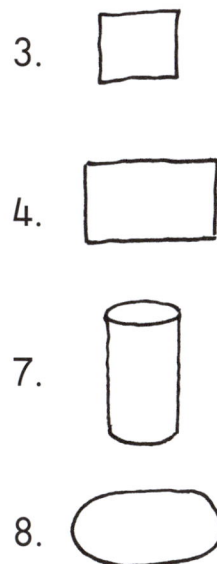

4.

7.

8.

Down

1.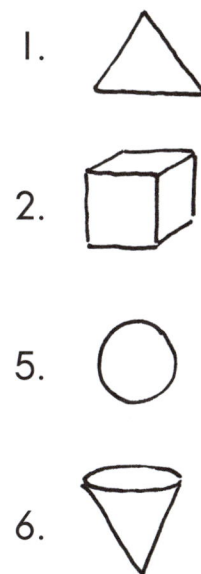

2.

5.

6.

7 ✏ Use a more interesting word than *looked* in each sentence.

The sailor _____ at the horizon for hours.

I _____ inside the box, hoping to find jewels and money.

8 ✏ Write your own sentences using these verbs.

glimpsed	_____
glanced	_____

Unit 28

The big red spot on the planet Jupiter is a **gigantic** storm. It's three times the size of Earth, and hundreds of years old!

Say Listen Look Understand Remember Practise

gather _____

garden _____

gentle _____

genius _____

giant _____

golden _____

guest _____

guide _____

garage _____

garbage _____

gigantic _____

gypsy _____

1 Say each list word aloud and listen to the sound the **g** makes. Write the word inside the appropriate shape.

soft **g** as in germ

_____
_____
_____
_____

hard **g** as in got

_____
_____
_____
_____

soft **g** and hard **g**

_____
_____
_____

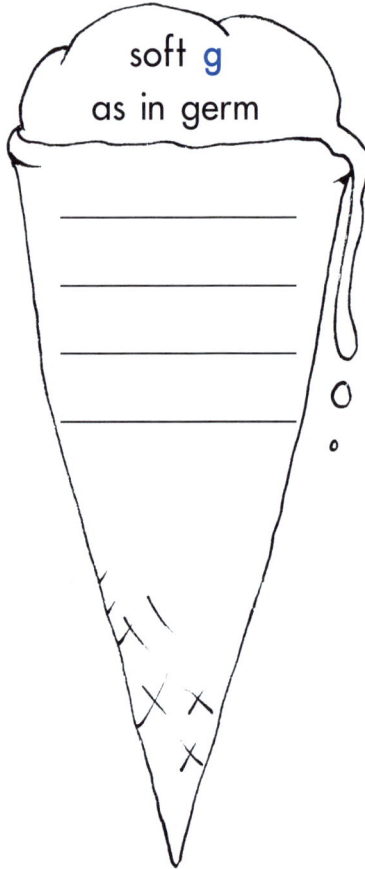

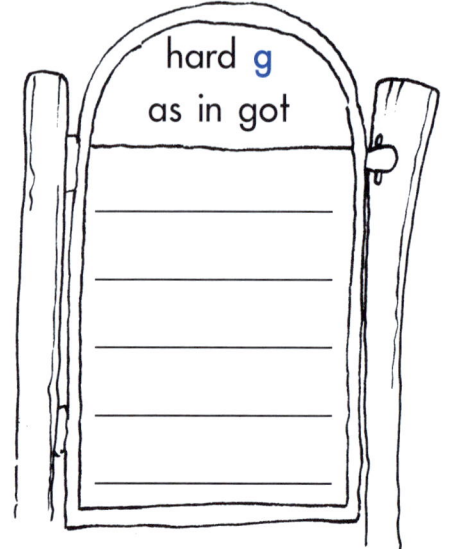

2 Look at the words in the ice-cream cone and on the gate. Fill in the missing letters for the two rules.

g is usually soft when the next letter is __, __ or __.

g is usually hard when the next letter is __, __ or __.

3 Say these words aloud. Put a tick in the box if they follow the rules above. Put a cross in the box if they don't.

gather ☐   golf ☐   gift ☐   generally ☐

giggle ☐   gaze ☐   guard ☐   gymnastics ☐

60   Soft and hard g sounds; soft g sound before e, i, y

4 Make a new word by adding a suffix from the box.

| ly   ed   er   th   ful   ing |

grace_____   guess_____   grow_____

glad_____   garden_____   groan_____

5 Make an adjective by adding **y**.
Take care if the word ends in **e**!

noun	adjective
greed	
gloom	
guilt	
grease	
gloss	

6 Complete the table.

singular	plural
gypsy	
grocery	
guest	
genius	
gentleman	

7 Here are some interesting words you can use instead of *big* and *little*.
Write the name of an animal that fits each adjective.

a gigantic _____   a microscopic _____

a giant _____   a minuscule _____

an enormous _____   a miniature _____

a huge _____   a tiny _____

a large _____   a midget _____

Unit 29

The Atlantic giant **squ**id has the biggest eyes of any creature. One squid had eyes 50 cm in diameter.

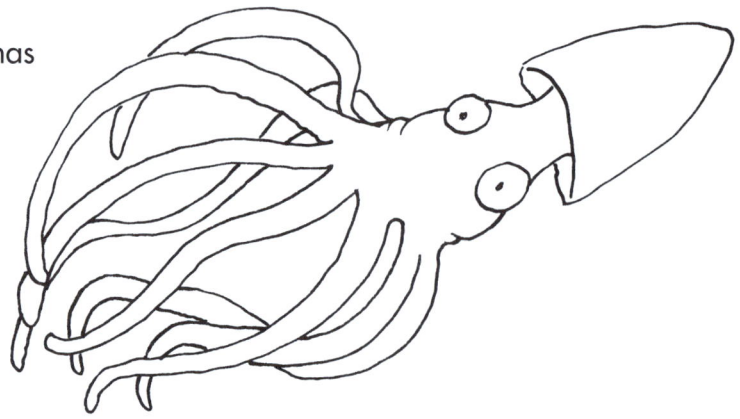

Say **L**isten **L**ook **U**nderstand **R**emember **P**ractise

quiet _____

quite _____

queue _____

quarter _____

s**qu**ash _____

s**qu**eal _____

s**qu**awk _____

s**qu**are _____

e**qu**al _____

re**qu**est _____

s**qu**irrel _____

mos**qu**ito _____

Rule!
- **q** is always followed by **u**.
- **qu** is always followed by another vowel.
- **cw** and **qw** do not go together in English.

1 👁 Fill in the missing vowels to make list words.

sq _ _ r _   _ q _ _ l

q _ _ _ t   q _ _ t _

sq _ _ _ l   q _ _ rt _ r

q _ _ _ _   r _ q _ _ st

2 👁 Use your dictionary to find these words starting with s**qu**.

1. | S | Q | U | | | | |
2. | S | Q | U | | | |
3. | S | Q | U | | | |
4. | S | Q | U | | | |
5. | S | Q | U | | | |
6. | S | Q | U | | | |
7. | S | Q | U | | | |
8. | S | Q | U | | | |
9. | S | Q | U | | | |

1. small furry animal
2. press together
3. look with eyes partly closed
4. sea animals with long tentacles
5. short high sound
6. crouch with a straight back
7. sound a parrot makes
8. shapes with four equal sides
9. line with twists or curves

3 Add suffixes to these verbs.

squash
- es _____
- ed _____
- ing _____

squirm
- s _____
- ed _____
- ing _____

4 Write the plural form for these insects.

ant _____   fly _____   mosquito _____

flea _____   wasp _____   cockroach _____

Tip!
These three words do not sound the same, so they are not homophones.
Yet some people do mix them up.

quit = stop   **quiet** = not loud   **quite** = completely

---

5 Colour the correct word.

The only time my brother is | quit | quiet | quite | is when he is asleep.

My brother asked me to | quit | quiet | quite | making such a racket.

My project is not | quit | quiet | quite | ready, so I'll bring it tomorrow.

6 Choose a word to complete each sentence.

> inquired   requested   questioned   demanded

Mum _____ a seat by the window when she booked her ticket.

Mr Lee _____ about his watch at the lost property office.

The police _____ the driver about the accident.

"I want my money back!" _____ the angry customer.

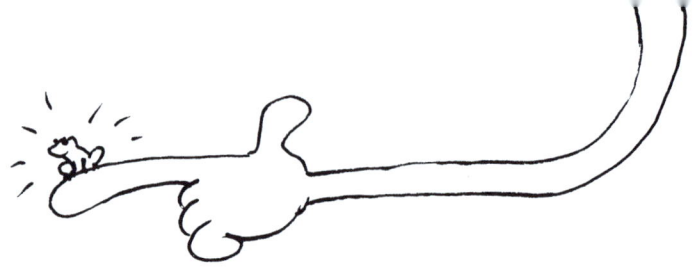

Unit 30

The world's smallest frog is from Cuba. It is just 8.5 **milli**metres long.

Say Listen Look Understand Remember Practise
metre _____
kilometre _____
centimetre _____
millimetre _____
litre _____
gram _____
decade _____
decimal _____
euro _____
uniform _____
bicycle _____
triangle _____

1 ✏️ Write the list word which is most appropriate for measuring each quantity.

weight of an orange _____

distance between cities _____

cost of a bus ride _____

height of a person _____

quantity of water _____

length of a ruler _____

length of an ant _____

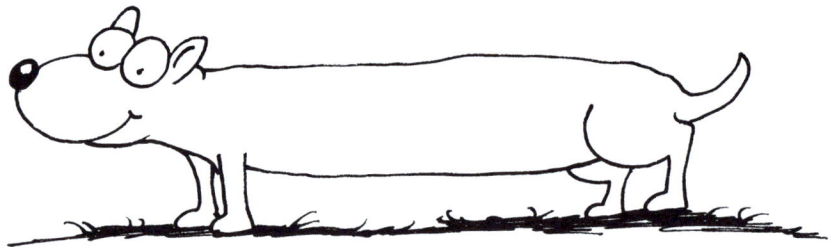

⭐ Tip! **Some prefixes indicate quantity.**

prefix	quantity	example
uni	1	unicycle
bi	2	biplane
tri	3	tricycle
quart	4	quarter

prefix	quantity	example
oct	8	octagon
dec	10	decade
centi	100	centimetre
milli	1000	millimetre

2 ✍️ Choose a word ending for each prefix.

pede	form	agon	er	cycle	opus	imal	angle

uni_____ bi_____ tri_____ quart_____

oct_____ dec_____ oct_____ milli_____

3 Write the full word for these abbreviations and symbols.
Then write in the circle the number of syllables in each word.

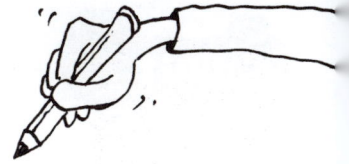

km _____ ◯   cm _____ ◯

mm _____ ◯   l _____ ◯

ml _____ ◯   kg _____ ◯

g _____ ◯   € _____ ◯

4 Write as many words as you can starting with each prefix. A dictionary will help.

uni	bi	tri
1	2	3

5 The letters of most of these words have been jumbled up. Write the sentences correctly.

I ma het olny mebmer of my faimly bron tihs cnetruy.

_____

We hnug ornage rtinagles on eth fecnes to mrak het tarck.

_____

6 All the vowels have been lost from this sentence. Write the sentence correctly.

Sm njys mths bt sms wth dcmls cnfs hm.

_____

Prefixes uni-, bi-, tri-, kilo-, dec-, centi-, milli-; topic words: measurement   65

In English, the writing goes from left to right. In Arabic, the writing goes from right to left. In Japanese, the writing goes from top to bottom, in columns.

1 Write the missing vowel sounds. The clues will help you.

c _ c _ mb _ r   long and green

b _ c _ cl _   it's fun to ride

g _ _ st   visitor to your home

q _ _ rt _ r   four make a whole

_ sl _ nd   land surrounded by water

m _ sq _ _ t _   biting insect

c _ l _ nd _ r   long, round shape

_ q _ _ l   same amount

r _ q _ _ st   polite question

a _ t _ _ n   the season between summer and winter

2 These words have lost their silent letters! Write them correctly.

thum _____

gost _____

onest _____

casle _____

nuckle _____

rong _____

riggle _____

rist _____

nife _____

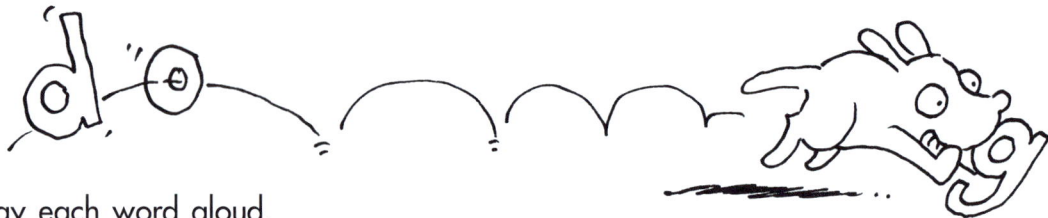

3 Say each word aloud.
Draw a circle around the **c** or **g** if it makes a soft sound as in *cent* or *giraffe*.
Draw a square around the **c** or **g** if it makes a hard sound as in *cat* or *goat*.

correct   cancel   garbage   guilty

bicycle   gentle   century   garage

calendar   certain   grammar   cement

4 The missing letters all make a **j** sound. Fill in **g** or **j**.

_ uicy   _ ymnasium   _ iraffe   _ ewel

_ inger   _ olly   _ iant   _ enius

_ azz   _ igantic   _ ourney   _ enerally

5 Make word families by adding prefixes and/or suffixes to these base words. If you need help, look in a dictionary.

honest   _____   _____   _____

doubt   _____   _____   _____

decide   _____   _____   _____

quiet   _____   _____   _____

garden   _____   _____   _____

6 Complete each sentence using a word from the box.

> quiet   quite

The crowd stopped shouting as the tennis player stepped up to the service line. Suddenly it was _____ and I was _____ surprised to realise I was holding my breath.

> we're   were   where

"Pack your bag quickly as _____ going away for the weekend!" Mum announced. This was news to me! _____ would we stay?

What _____ we going to do? I knew I would find out soon.

7 Find anagrams for these words.

plum _____   asleep _____

seam _____   cares _____

sword _____   bruise _____

listen _____   fluster _____

If the wind is cold enough and strong enough, icicles grow sideways.

Say Listen Look Understand Remember Practise

simple	_____
trouble	_____
horrible	_____
terrible	_____
jungle	_____
tangle	_____
icicle	_____
tentacle	_____
spectacles	_____
tickle	_____
hurdle	_____
whistle	_____

Tip! Words with double consonants in the middle always have more than one syllable. There is a syllable break between the consonants. hor/ri/ble

1 Draw lines to show the syllables in these words. For example: jun/gle

simple	trouble
terrible	tangle
icicle	tentacle
spectacles	tickle
hurdle	whistle

2 Do these words end in **le** or **el**? Write the missing letters.

kenn _ _   tick _ _   lab _ _   hurd _ _   tunn _ _

3 Make list words by changing or leaving out the circled letters.

s(a)mple _____   t(i)ngle _____

t(r)ickle _____   (t)histle _____

(b)ungle _____   bic(y)cle _____

hu(d)dle _____   (b)angle _____

4 ✎ Make words with a silent **t**. Underline all the silent letters.

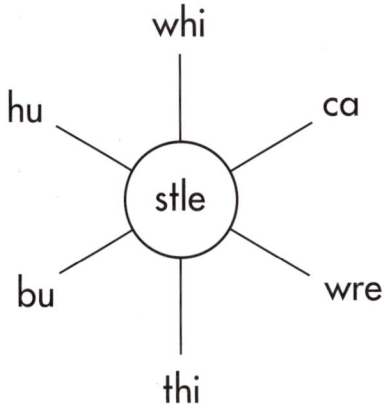

whi
hu   ca
   stle
bu   wre
thi

_____   _____

_____   _____

_____   _____

5 ✎ The words in the box form a part of something bigger. Write each word in the box next to the word it belongs to.

| tentacle   lenses   handle   spout   stirrup   knuckle |

saddle _____   spectacles _____   octopus _____

finger _____   kettle _____   knife _____

6 ✎ Use the clues to find the mystery word.
Tip: All of the words end in **le**.

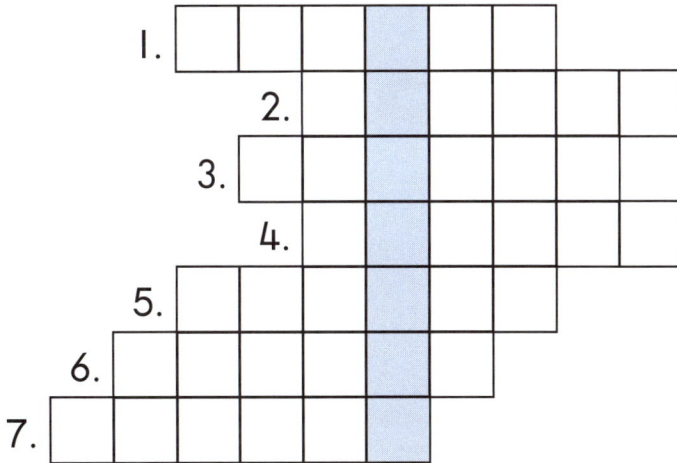

1.
2.
3.
4.
5.
6.
7.

1. sea creature with a shell on its back
2. three lots of
3. plural of person
4. colour
5. two lots of
6. one lot of
7. not complicated

Try to stay out of this! _____

7 ✎ Write one or two sentences using these words.

| horrible | _____ |
| terrible | _____ |

The first living creature to go on a space mission was Laika the dog, in 1957.

Say Listen Look Understand Remember Practise	
station	_____
nation	_____
fiction	_____
section	_____
fraction	_____
cushion	_____
fashion	_____
mission	_____
religion	_____
million	_____
billion	_____
champion	_____

1 ✎ Write list words.

A millionaire is someone who has a _____ euro.

A billionaire is someone who has a _____ euro.

I'll meet you at the train _____.

I am going to be a _____ swimmer.

One-quarter is a _____.

I'd like to be an astronaut on a space _____.

2 ✎ Would you look in the fiction or non-fiction section for these books?

A History of Our Nation   _non-fiction section_

Life on a Space Station _____

Charlie Cheers the Champions _____

The Pyramids of Ancient Egypt _____

3 👁 Write a list word to match each shape.

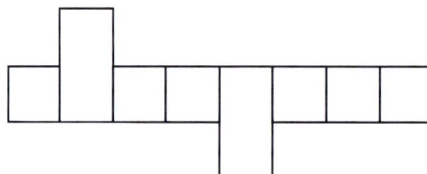

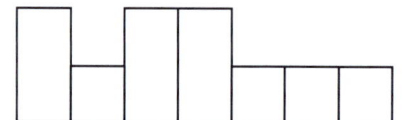

4 There has been a word explosion. Find a noun to match each verb.

preparation
exploration
imagination
separation
explanation
organisation
occupation
operation

verb	noun
imagine	
explore	
occupy	
prepare	
operate	
organise	
explain	
separate	

5 Find the **ion** words in the trophy and write them in the **suffix added** column. Write the verb that belongs to the same word family as the noun.

mountaincertainiron
suspicionmusician
curtaininformationjoin
decisionaim
maintaincontainerexplosion

Base word (verb)   **Suffix added**

_____   _____

_____   _____

_____   _____

_____   _____

6 Use both rhyming words in one sentence.

fashion
passion

_____

_____

The largest **pizza** ever baked measured 37.4 m in diameter.

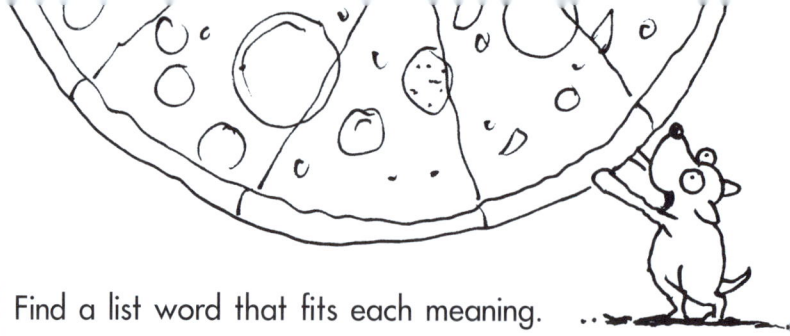

Say Listen Look Understand Remember Practise

igloo	_____
robot	_____
yacht	_____
iceberg	_____
khaki	_____
tsunami	_____
kindergarten	_____
pizza	_____
spaghetti	_____
banshee	_____
chocolate	_____
restaurant	_____

1 Find a list word that fits each meaning.

An Inuit (Eskimo) word meaning **house**

_____

A Hindi (Indian) word meaning **dusty**

_____

A Japanese word meaning **harbour wave**

_____

A German word meaning **child's garden**

_____

An Irish word meaning **woman of the fairy mound**

_____

2 Here are some Italian words. Which ones can you eat? Which ones can you drink?

cappuccino
pizza
spaghetti
latte
ravioli
broccoli
risotto
salami

Eat:

_____

_____

Drink:

_____

_____

3 **Restaurant** is a French word now used in many languages. Look it up in your dictionary and write its meaning.

restaurant_____

4 ✏️ Write the list word you might find in these locations.

The Antarctic Ocean _____

A factory handling dangerous chemicals _____

A marina _____

A sweet shop _____

At a restaurant _____

⭐ **Tip!** **Desert** and **dessert** are often confused, even though they are not homophones.
desert = hot, dry place
dessert = sweet food

I'd like a second serve of dessert!

5 👂 Colour the correct word.

It is often cold at night in the | desert | dessert |.

My favourite | desert | dessert | is jelly and ice-cream.

6 👁️ Colour the correct homophone.

We used a | course | coarse | sieve to remove the small pebbles.

Dad has just finished a training | course | coarse | for cricket umpires.

7 ✏️ Write a paragraph about eating a meal in a restaurant.
Use these words: *restaurant, menu, course.*

_____

_____

_____

_____

_____

_____

Some experts say the average adult speaks 12,500 words a day.

woof

1 Complete the tables.

adjective	adverb
quick	
	quietly
smooth	
	happily

noun	adjective
happiness	
sadness	
	dreamy
	stripy

Holy adjectives...
It's the homophone!

2 Write the homophone for each word.

coarse _____

hole _____

peace _____

night _____

steel _____

blue _____

new _____

tyre _____

wait _____

sure _____

brake _____

write _____

stair _____

threw _____

rap _____

guessed _____

allowed _____

site _____

3 Homographs have the same spelling but more than one meaning. Give two meanings for each of these words.

cricket 1. _____ 2. _____

pupil 1. _____ 2. _____

coach 1. _____ 2. _____

match 1. _____ 2. _____

4 ✏️ Words ending in **e** drop the **e** before adding **y**. Make an adjective by adding **y** to these words.

shade _____   stripe _____

stone _____   wriggle _____

cuddle _____   lace _____

ice _____   taste _____

5 👁️ Make a new word by adding a letter.

save _____ (cut off beard)   piece _____ (stick into)

hose _____ (an animal)   word _____ (Earth)

steam _____ (small river)   truck _____ (hit)

quit _____ (bed cover)   tale _____ (not fresh)

6 👁️ Change one letter to make a new word.

suction _____ (a part)   worm _____ (group of letters)

green _____ (say hello)   sample _____ (easy)

pedal _____ (an award)   candle _____ (hold it)

belief _____ (end of worries)   fresh _____ (meat)

project _____ (look after)   carry _____ (Indian spice)

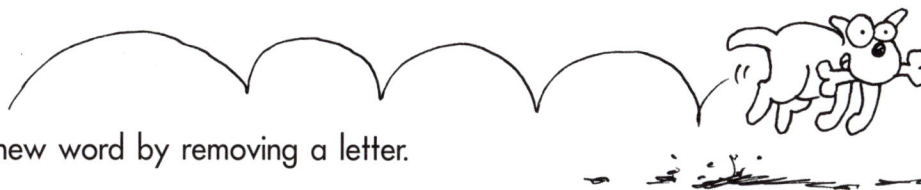

7 👁️ Make a new word by removing a letter.

strain _____ (transport)   grain _____ (get more)

violent _____ (colour)   learn _____ (get money)

craft _____ (it floats)   barrow _____ (goes with bow)

brain _____ (healthy food)   bend _____ (finish)

LIST WORDS IN UNIT ORDER

Unit 1
care
made
table
place
shade
awake
time
slice
stripe
while
white
alive

Unit 2
home
stone
close
whole
alone
gone
love
done
use
pure
huge
cube

Unit 3
tool
shook
blood
street
sweep
dream
head
beach
great
paint
road
float

Unit 4
grow
throw
below
ground

found
proud
mountain
enjoy
money
honey
delay
away

Unit 5
across
always
about
around
almost
already
ahead
asleep
above
another
along
altogether

Unit 7
shouting
baking
beginning
emptying
bumped
screamed
dropped
invited
worried
crossly
happily
lovely

Unit 8
Ireland
county
Belfast
Dublin
Donegal
Cork
Galway
Kildare
Limerick

Meath
Tipperary
Sligo

Unit 9
bigger
hotter
nicer
closer
higher
larger
happier
cheapest
fastest
loudest
fittest
funniest

Unit 10
brief
grief
relief
fielder
fierce
shield
niece
piece
sieve
thieve
believe
friend

Unit 11
untidy
unlikely
mischief
misplace
misbehave
mistake
disagree
disgrace
disgusting
dishonest
disobey
discover

Unit 13
Christmas
angel
shepherd
donkey
manger
carol
holly
wreath
present
stocking
reindeer
celebrate

Unit 14
joyful
useful
playful
cheerful
helpful
awful
careful
painful
peaceful
colourful
grateful
beautiful

Unit 15
less
hopeless
harmless
heartless
fearless
press
grass
guess
express
progress
compass
princess

Unit 16
letter
butter
gallop
balloon

kennel
tunnel
tennis
rubbish
summer
lesson
blossom
burrow

Unit 17
apple
saddle
puddle
riddle
cuddle
bubble
bottle
kettle
little
juggle
giggle
wriggle

Unit 18
January
February
March
April
May
June
July
August
September
October
November
December

Unit 20
sigh
sight
might
bright
midnight
frighten
knight
eight
neigh

76

weight
sleigh
neighbour

Unit 21
tough
rough
cough
enough
though
thought
bought
fought
taught
caught
daughter
naughty

Unit 22
sadness
happiness
revision
television
direction
friendship
kingdom
freedom
forward
backward
childhood
neighbourhood

Unit 23
toe
canoe
tomato
potato
mango
hero
piano
kangaroo
dozen
women
trousers
scissors

Unit 24

puff
cliff
staff
shelf
half
wolf
scarf
leaf
knife
themselves
handkerchief
giraffe

Unit 26
wrap
wrinkle
kneel
calm
castle
comb
island
honest
tongue
autumn
doubt
ghost

Unit 27
carpet
cancel
cent
once
city
correct
cure
lettuce
cucumber
cylinder
because
decide

Unit 28
gather
garden
gentle
genius
giant

golden
guest
guide
garage
garbage
gigantic
gypsy

Unit 29
quiet
quite
queue
quarter
squash
squeal
squawk
square
equal
request
squirrel
mosquito

Unit 30
metre
kilometre
centimetre
millimetre
litre
gram
decade
decimal
euro
uniform
bicycle
triangle

Unit 32
simple
trouble
horrible
terrible
jungle
tangle
icicle
tentacle
spectacles
tickle

hurdle
whistle

Unit 33
station
nation
fiction
section
fraction
cushion
fashion
mission
religion
million
billion
champion

Unit 34
igloo
robot
yacht
iceberg
khaki
tsunami
kindergarten
pizza
spaghetti
gelato
chocolate
restaurant

77

LIST WORDS IN ALPHABETICAL ORDER

about	Unit 5	butter	Unit 16
above	Unit 5		
across	Unit 5	calm	Unit 26
ahead	Unit 5	cancel	Unit 27
alive	Unit 1	canoe	Unit 23
almost	Unit 5	care	Unit 1
alone	Unit 2	careful	Unit 14
along	Unit 5	carol	Unit 13
already	Unit 5	carpet	Unit 27
altogether	Unit 5	castle	Unit 26
always	Unit 5	caught	Unit 21
angel	Unit 13	celebrate	Unit 13
another	Unit 5	cent	Unit 27
apple	Unit 17	centimetre	Unit 30
April	Unit 18	champion	Unit 33
around	Unit 5	cheapest	Unit 9
asleep	Unit 5	cheerful	Unit 14
August	Unit 18	childhood	Unit 22
Australia	Unit 8	chocolate	Unit 34
autumn	Unit 26	Christmas	Unit 13
awake	Unit 1	city	Unit 27
away	Unit 4	cliff	Unit 24
awful	Unit 14	close	Unit 2
		closer	Unit 9
backward	Unit 22	colourful	Unit 14
baking	Unit 7	comb	Unit 26
balloon	Unit 16	compass	Unit 15
banshee	Unit 34	Cork	Unit 8
beach	Unit 3	correct	Unit 27
beautiful	Unit 14	cough	Unit 21
because	Unit 27	county	Unit 8
beginning	Unit 7	crossly	Unit 7
Belfast	Unit 8	cube	Unit 2
believe	Unit 10	cucumber	Unit 27
below	Unit 4	cuddle	Unit 17
bicycle	Unit 30	cure	Unit 27
bigger	Unit 9	cushion	Unit 33
billion	Unit 33	cylinder	Unit 27
blood	Unit 3		
blossom	Unit 16	daughter	Unit 21
bottle	Unit 17	decade	Unit 30
bought	Unit 21	December	Unit 18
brief	Unit 10	decide	Unit 27
bright	Unit 20	decimal	Unit 30
bubble	Unit 17	delay	Unit 4
bumped	Unit 7	direction	Unit 22
burrow	Unit 16	disagree	Unit 11

discover	Unit 11	genius	Unit 28
disgrace	Unit 11	gentle	Unit 28
disgusting	Unit 11	ghost	Unit 26
dishonest	Unit 11	giant	Unit 28
disobey	Unit 11	gigantic	Unit 28
done	Unit 2	giggle	Unit 17
Donegal	Unit 8	giraffe	Unit 24
donkey	Unit 13	golden	Unit 28
doubt	Unit 26	gone	Unit 2
dozen	Unit 23	gram	Unit 30
dream	Unit 3	grass	Unit 15
dropped	Unit 7	grateful	Unit 14
Dublin	Unit 8	great	Unit 3
		grief	Unit 10
eight	Unit 20	ground	Unit 4
emptying	Unit 7	grow	Unit 4
enjoy	Unit 4	guess	Unit 15
enough	Unit 21	guest	Unit 28
equal	Unit 29	guide	Unit 28
euro	Unit 29	gypsy	Unit 28
express	Unit 15		
		half	Unit 24
fashion	Unit 33	handkerchief	Unit 24
fastest	Unit 9	happier	Unit 9
fearless	Unit 15	happily	Unit 7
February	Unit 18	happiness	Unit 22
fiction	Unit 33	harmless	Unit 15
fielder	Unit 10	head	Unit 3
fierce	Unit 10	heartless	Unit 15
fittest	Unit 9	helpful	Unit 14
float	Unit 3	hero	Unit 23
forward	Unit 22	higher	Unit 9
fought	Unit 21	holly	Unit 13
found	Unit 34	home	Unit 2
fraction	Unit 32	honest	Unit 26
freedom	Unit 22	honey	Unit 4
friend	Unit 10	hopeless	Unit 15
friendship	Unit 22	horrible	Unit 32
frighten	Unit 20	hotter	Unit 9
funniest	Unit 9	huge	Unit 2
		hurdle	Unit 32
gallop	Unit 16		
Galway	Unit 8	iceberg	Unit 34
garage	Unit 28	icicle	Unit 32
garbage	Unit 28	igloo	Unit 34
garden	Unit 28	invited	Unit 7
gather	Unit 28	Ireland	Unit 8

SPELLING RULES AND TIPS

To make a plural

If a noun ends in **o**, the plural usually ends in **es**.
  echo → *echoes*

If the word ends in two vowels, just add **s**.
  kangaroo → *kangaroos*   *radio* → *radios*

If a noun ends in **f** or **fe**, change the **f** or **fe** to **v** and add **es** to form the plural.
  elf → *elves*   *life* → *lives*

If a noun ends in **ff** or **ffe**, add **s** to form the plural.
  cliff → *cliffs*   *giraffe* → *giraffes*

Past tense

Most verbs show the past tense by adding **ed**.
  discover → *discovered*

Some verbs have a different form in the past tense.
  write → *wrote*

Adding ful and ness

If a word ends with a short **y**, change **y** to **i** before adding **ful**.
  beauty → *beautiful*

If an adjective ends with a short **y**, change the **y** to **i** before adding **ness**.
  happy → *happiness*

Proper nouns name people, places, days of the week, months etc.
Proper nouns are always written with a capital letter.
  Nuala   Spain   Wednesday   October

Synonyms are words with similar meanings.
  Small and *little* are synonyms.

Antonyms are words with the opposite meaning.
  Full and *empty* are antonyms.
Antonyms can be formed using prefixes and suffixes.
  *kind   **un**kind   harm**ful**   harm**less***

Use an **apostrophe** to show that someone owns something.
  Tim's bag

An **anagram** is formed by rearranging the letters in a word.
  Lemon is an anagram of *melon*.